coloryourselfsmart
Dinosaurs

The fun, visual way to teach yourself about anything and everything

By Dominic Couzens

Illustrations by David Nurney

THUNDER BAY
P · R · E · S · S

San Diego, California

Thunder Bay Press
An imprint of the Baker & Taylor Publishing Group
10350 Barnes Canyon Road, San Diego, CA 92121
www.thunderbaybooks.com

All notations of errors or omissions should be addressed to Thunder Bay Press, Editorial Department, at the above address. All other correspondence (author inquiries, permissions) concerning the content of this book should be addressed to HarperCollins Publishers, 77–85 Fulham Palace Rd, London, W6 8JB, U.K.

ISBN-13: 978-1-60710-573-2
ISBN-10: 1-60710-573-X

Printed in China

1 2 3 4 5 15 14 13 12

CONTENTS

INTRODUCTION 4
About the Color Yourself Smart Series
How to Use This Book
Colored Pencil Techniques

LATE TRIASSIC 10
Plateosaurus
Herrerasaurus
Eudimorphodon
Saurosuchus
Coelophysis

EARLY TO MID-JURASSIC . . . 20
Massospondylus
Scelidosaurus
Rhomaleosaurus
Gongxianosaurus
Megalosaurus

LATE JURASSIC 30
Mamenchisaurus
Huayangosaurus
Stegosaurus
Diplodocus
Brachiosaurus
Kentrosaurus
Camarasaurus
Archaeopteryx
Allosaurus

EARLY CRETACEOUS 48
Iguanodon
Ouranosaurus
Gastonia
Utahraptor
Deinonychus
Microraptor
Sinosauropteryx
Tupandactylus
Amargasaurus
Archaeoceratops
Argentinosaurus

LATE CRETACEOUS 70
Quetzalcoatlus
Spinosaurus
Carcharodontosaurus
Tyrannosaurus
Triceratops
Velociraptor
Protoceratops
Pachycephalosaurus
Chasmosaurus
Torosaurus
Pentaceratops
Psittacosaurus
Lambeosaurus
Parasaurolophus
Maiasaura

Ankylosaurus
Oviraptor
Troodon
Majungasaurus
Saltasaurus
Therizinosaurus
Centrosaurus

**DINOSAURS IN
FULL COLOR** 114

QUIZ 127
Quiz
Quiz Answers

INTRODUCTION

"DINOSAURS"—THE VERY WORD CONJURES UP THRILLING IMAGES OF GIANT MONSTERS FROM AN UNIMAGINABLY LONG TIME PAST. These creatures have held people in their thrall ever since the term "Dinosauria" was coined in 1842, and there is no sign of the dinosaur craze abating today—in fact, quite the reverse. In the last 30 years, a suite of new techniques for the study of fossils has become available. This scientific advance, paired with a seemingly never-ending succession of eye-catching finds swelling the fossil records, means that the golden age of dinosaur appreciation—if not the zenith of the animals themselves—is now.

It is remarkable that we should be so familiar with animals that died out, at the very least, 65 million years ago. That we are is a tribute to the many men and women who have identified bones and other material, dug them up, and pieced them together to re-create a lost world from these splintered remains. What they are working on is essentially one of the world's most absorbing detective stories: tiny discoveries uncover big facts, and stories are created by these impossibly ancient clues.

This book is designed to help you learn about 52 species of dinosaurs by coloring in their depictions. Each portrait has ten labels telling you things that you can see, or sometimes infer, from the illustration. Each species also has a brief introduction on the facing page. By drawing together all these threads, you will gain a few insights into what makes each dinosaur different from the rest, as well as why it is interesting or unusual.

You might not think that the word "dinosaur" needs an explanation, but actually it does, and there are a few creatures included in this book that are not technically dinosaurs at all—such as a few pterosaurs (flying reptiles). To be a card-carrying dinosaur, a reptile needed to have a particular arrangement of its hip and leg bones, causing its limbs to be held directly beneath the body, rather than sprawling out to the side. There are also other aspects of the skeleton that unify dinosaurs, but many are extremely complicated and arcane. Recently, it has been fully realized that modern-day birds are direct descendents of dinosaurs, fully fitting the official anatomical description.

Overall, about 600 species of dinosaurs have been described from their fossil remains, and they broadly fit into three main groups. The sauropods include the famous long-necked, small-headed giants such as Brachiosaurus; the theropods include the bipedal monster carnivores such as Tyrannosaurus, as well as the birdlike dinosaurs such as raptors; and the ornithischians includes the armored dinosaurs such as Stegosaurus and Triceratops.

The age of dinosaurs lasted from about 250 to 65 million years ago. It came in gradually as animals evolved into dinosaurs, but ended brutally and quickly, when, many scientists believe, an asteroid strike in the Gulf of Mexico wiped out all the dinosaurs (the so-called K-T extinction), apart from the birds. The time from 250–65 million years ago (mya) is called the Mesozoic era, and it is divided into three main periods: the Triassic (250–200 mya), Jurassic (199–145 mya), and Cretaceous (145–65 mya), each with its own geological profile. Dinosaurs can be dated from the rocks in which their fossils are found, and for convenience, in this book we have grouped together dinosaurs from the same period. Experts have no conclusive evidence of dinosaurs' true colors, so the colors used in the final illustrations are for interpretation only. Feel free to make your own interpretations, based on ideas of camouflage, habitat, and diet.

The idea of this book, then, is to color in and learn about the dinosaurs in a fun way. And once you have colored in all 52 plates, try the quiz at the end, which you might find challenging. Overall, we hope that this book enhances your enjoyment of these prehistoric marvels.

ABOUT THE
COLOR YOURSELF SMART
SERIES

COLOR YOURSELF SMART is a revolutionary new series designed to help improve your memory and make learning easy. Leading memory and learning experts agree that color and illustrations help reinforce difficult subject matter and greatly increase your chances of both creating visual memories and recalling that information faster. So if you find it difficult to remember something—even after you've just read it—then it's time to start coloring your way to faster learning and a sharper memory!

OTHER BOOKS IN THE SERIES:

Color Yourself Smart: Geography
Color Yourself Smart: Human Anatomy
Color Yourself Smart: Birds of North America
Color Yourself Smart: Masterpieces of Art

HOW TO USE THIS BOOK

A pack of eight artists' studio-quality coloring pencils from Faber-Castell is included with this book; however, you should feel free to supplement these colors with your own as you see fit—the more colors you have available to you, the more enjoyable you will find memorizing the material. A colored plate section is included at the back of the book, showing all of the featured illustrations colored in for your reference, and a color key accompanies those illustrations that are more complicated in nature, for readers who prefer a little more guidance.

Keep your pencil tips pointed with the accompanying sharpener, and use the eraser to blend or to erase any mishaps. The eraser is more effective when used on lighter washes of color and may not be so helpful if you have pressed too hard with one of the darker colors.

COLORED PENCIL TECHNIQUES

Numerous finishes can be achieved with colored pencils, depending on how they are used. Artists' quality pencils can be smudged for a watercolor effect, and different colors can be blended to create other colors. When blending pencil colors, it is best to lay down the lighter color first and overlay the darker colors to achieve the desired effect.

Pressing harder or lighter on the paper will also give a different shade of color. It is easier to use the side of a pencil point to wash large areas with color and to use a sharp point for those areas that require more careful coloring or more detail.

Plateosaurus | *Plateosaurus longiceps*

Late Triassic, Europe • 216–203 million years ago • 26 feet (8 m) long

AT FIRST SIGHT, THIS PLATEOSAURUS does not seem to be doing anything remarkable—just rearing up on its hind legs to graze on the foliage of a tree fern. But this is the late Triassic period, about 210 million years ago, at the very beginning of the history of the dinosaurs. Until Plateosaurus, all large herbivores had been restricted to feeding on the ground, but this exceptional animal is thought to have been the first to be able to reach the upper branches of trees. As a result, it was enormously successful and became one of the most abundant Triassic dinosaurs.

One intriguing feature of this dinosaur's biology is that it seems to have shown great variation in adult size. Some preserved specimens are 16.5 feet (5 m) long, while others are as big as 33 feet (10 m) long; evidently, the difference was related to diet and general health. Plateosaurus certainly lived in an unpredictable environment, with seasonally dry conditions. Some dinosaur experts think that it might have migrated in herds at certain times of the year to look for abundant plant growth, since fossils are highly concentrated in a few places.

Plateosaurus is classified with a group called the prosauropods. These creatures developed before the large and dominant sauropod group, but they are not thought to be ancestors. Instead they lived alongside early sauropods before becoming extinct in the early Jurassic period—the first major group of dinosaurs to die out.

10 THINGS TO REMEMBER

1. Partially opposable thumbs on its forelimbs helped it grasp tree trunks and branches.

2. It had five fingers (two of which were very small), a primitive feature often shown by prosauropods.

3. The long neck was a newly evolved feature at the time—but appeared on many later giant sauropods, such as Brachiosaurus.

4. It had a relatively slender body compared with later sauropod giants.

5. It had fairly short limbs, especially its forelimbs.

6. Rearing up on two legs to browse high-growing plant material was a major step forward for dinosaurs.

7. It had a lightly built skull (primitive feature).

8. A long tail helped it balance when high browsing and walking.

9. It had a fairly heavy body, as its bones did not have many holes to decrease the weight.

10. Cycads (tree ferns) were a dominant feature of the Triassic landscape and would certainly have been eaten by Plateosaurus.

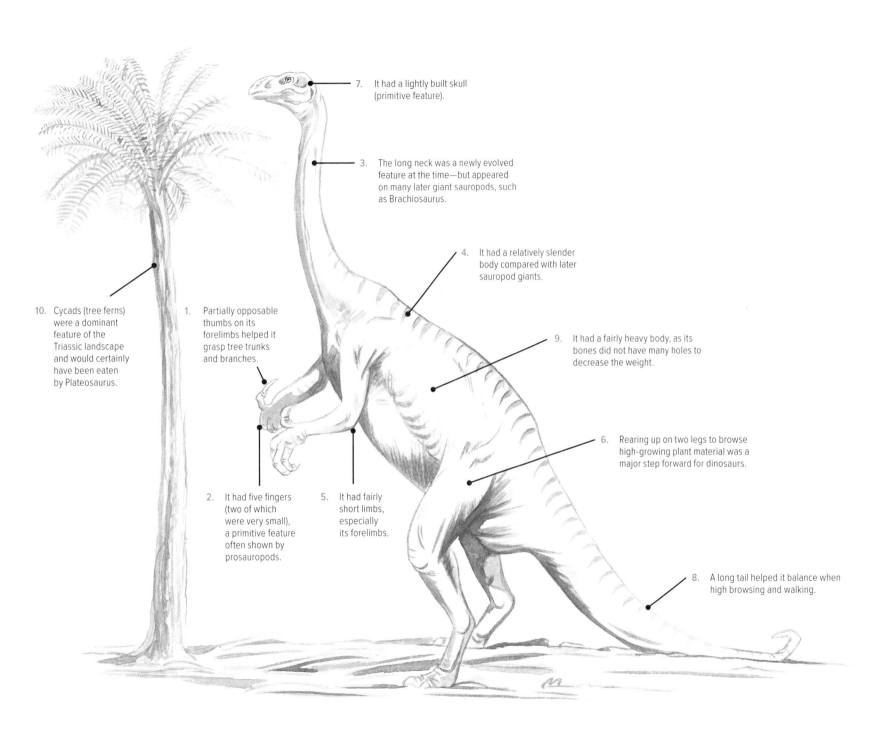

7. It had a lightly built skull (primitive feature).

3. The long neck was a newly evolved feature at the time—but appeared on many later giant sauropods, such as Brachiosaurus.

4. It had a relatively slender body compared with later sauropod giants.

10. Cycads (tree ferns) were a dominant feature of the Triassic landscape and would certainly have been eaten by Plateosaurus.

1. Partially opposable thumbs on its forelimbs helped it grasp tree trunks and branches.

9. It had a fairly heavy body, as its bones did not have many holes to decrease the weight.

6. Rearing up on two legs to browse high-growing plant material was a major step forward for dinosaurs.

2. It had five fingers (two of which were very small), a primitive feature often shown by prosauropods.

5. It had fairly short limbs, especially its forelimbs.

8. A long tail helped it balance when high browsing and walking.

Herrerasaurus | *Herrerasaurus ischigualastensis*

Late Triassic, Argentina • 230–217 million years ago • 15 feet (4.5 m) long

THE DISCOVERED EXISTENCE OF THIS PREDATORY, bipedal, and very ancient dinosaur has recently led experts to conclude something never before considered: that the first true dinosaurs evolved in South America. Herrerasaurus occurs in fossil deposits with several other very primitive dinosaurs, but the same sediments are heavily populated with fossils of thecodonts, the dominant reptiles of the time—in other words, these parent rocks have cataloged changing times. Modest in size, Herrerasaurus would have been preyed upon by the largest thecodonts, but by the end of the Triassic period, true dinosaurs would have surpassed their rivals in abundance and might, turning the tables.

Herrerasaurus was a large, fast-running pursuit predator that had serrated, bladelike teeth of 2 inches (5 cm) in length. It probably killed its prey by slashing at it and causing fatal wounds, either by glancing bites or grabs with its sharp claws, and in this way, it could probably overcome large animals. Its arms were very long, ideal for attacks involving reaching.

Many features of Herrerasaurus are primitive, including complicated aspects of the skeleton. It probably had only the beginnings of the efficient respiratory system seen in later theropods, and soon its direct descendants provided so much competition for food that Herrerasaurus became extinct.

10 THINGS TO REMEMBER

1. Hands had four fingers, a primitive trait.

2. Feet had five toes: four used for weight-bearing and one very small. This is another primitive trait.

3. Connection of femur to pelvis differed slightly from other dinosaurs, creating dispute as to whether or not it is a dinosaur at all.

4. Two-inch- (5-cm-) long teeth in jaw were shaped like serrated blades.

5. Claws on hands were sharp and probably able to deliver slashing blows to prey.

6. Long forelimbs would have allowed for good reach so that it could wound prey at a distance.

7. It had a slender, flexible neck.

8. Skull contained internal holes to reduce weight.

9. Long tail helped with balance when running.

10. Long snout may have enabled it to reach prey taking refuge in vegetation.

COLOR YOURSELF SMART
DINOSAURS LATE TRIASSIC

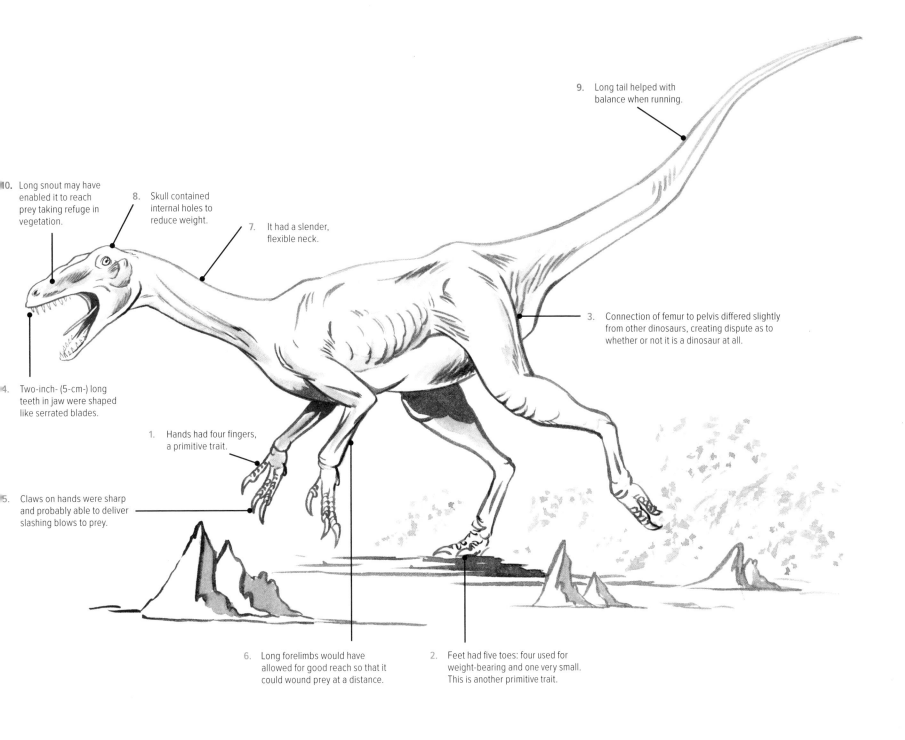

9. Long tail helped with balance when running.

10. Long snout may have enabled it to reach prey taking refuge in vegetation.

8. Skull contained internal holes to reduce weight.

7. It had a slender, flexible neck.

3. Connection of femur to pelvis differed slightly from other dinosaurs, creating dispute as to whether or not it is a dinosaur at all.

4. Two-inch- (5-cm-) long teeth in jaw were shaped like serrated blades.

1. Hands had four fingers, a primitive trait.

5. Claws on hands were sharp and probably able to deliver slashing blows to prey.

6. Long forelimbs would have allowed for good reach so that it could wound prey at a distance.

2. Feet had five toes: four used for weight-bearing and one very small. This is another primitive trait.

Eudimorphodon | *Eudimorphodon ranzii*

Late Triassic, Italy • 216–203 million years ago • Wingspan 3 feet (1 m)

FEW IMAGES OF THE MESOZOIC ERA, in textbooks or in film, appear without pterosaurs in the sky. These flying reptiles were contemporaries of the dinosaurs from the beginning to the end and are often considered to be dinosaurs. However, they are actually an entirely separate group classified by their different arrangement of leg bones. They predate the other flying vertebrates, such as birds and bats, by more than 100 million years. However, no one is certain about exactly how they flew—how much was powered flight, and how much was gliding.

If you trained your binoculars on Eudimorphodon, you would instantly recognize it as a primitive pterosaur by its long tail and extended toothed jaw—many later species lacked both tails and teeth. In fact, its teeth were extraordinary—there were 110 of them crammed into just 2 inches (5 cm) of jaw. At the front of the jaw were fangs that were much longer than the other teeth, and it seems highly likely that the fangs evolved in order to aid in grabbing fish from the water. There is little doubt that this small pterosaur was a fish eater, because the remains of fish have been found in its fossilized stomach remains.

Eudimorphodon is one of the earliest-known pterosaurs, flying through the Triassic skies more than 200 million years ago. Pterosaurs appear in the fossil record quite suddenly and fully formed, and it is a mystery as to how they evolved the power of flight.

10 THINGS TO REMEMBER

1. The long tail was free and flexible (later pterosaurs had rigid tails).

2. The diamond-shaped tail tip may have helped in steering.

3. Despite Eudimorphodon being an ancient fossil, its fish diet has been confirmed.

4. Long fangs at the front of the skull held onto its slippery fish prey, suggesting an active hunting style.

5. A pterosaur's wing was made up of a large flap connected to the fourth finger.

6. The fourth finger was very long.

7. Structure of the breastbone suggests that this pterosaur may have been able to flap its wings powerfully.

8. Protopagium was the flap of skin that formed the leading edge in flight.

9. Brachyopatagium was the main part of the wing; the trailing edge.

10. The long, narrow skull reduced air resistance.

14

DID YOU KNOW?

Some pterosaurs were able to fly at 75 miles per hour (120 km/h).

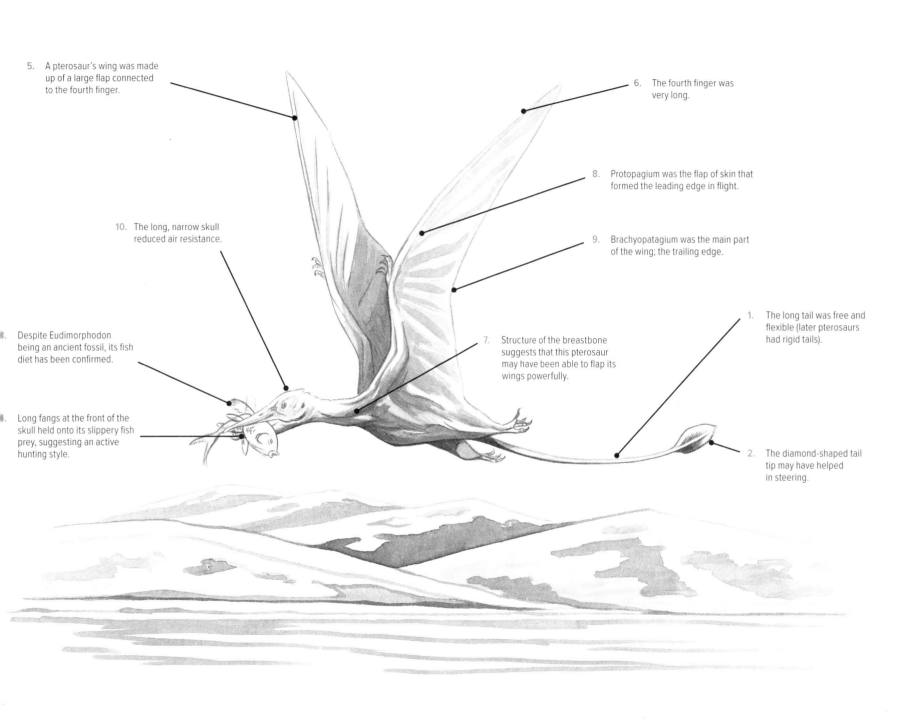

5. A pterosaur's wing was made up of a large flap connected to the fourth finger.

6. The fourth finger was very long.

8. Protopagium was the flap of skin that formed the leading edge in flight.

10. The long, narrow skull reduced air resistance.

9. Brachyopatagium was the main part of the wing; the trailing edge.

3. Despite Eudimorphodon being an ancient fossil, its fish diet has been confirmed.

7. Structure of the breastbone suggests that this pterosaur may have been able to flap its wings powerfully.

1. The long tail was free and flexible (later pterosaurs had rigid tails).

4. Long fangs at the front of the skull held onto its slippery fish prey, suggesting an active hunting style.

2. The diamond-shaped tail tip may have helped in steering.

Saurosuchus | *Saurosuchus galilei*

Late Triassic, Argentina • 230–217 million years ago • 23 feet (7 m) long

CROCODILES AND ALLIGATORS ARE INTIMIDATING ANIMALS at the best of times, but imagine coming across one that, rather than remaining idly on the riverbank, actually ran quickly on all fours to chase you. That gives you some idea of what was faced by the animals who shared the Triassic swamps of Argentina with the fearsome top predator Saurosuchus. Strictly speaking, Saurosuchus was not a dinosaur—or even a crocodilian; it was actually an early, lesser-known rauisuchian. For a time, these meat eaters filled the predatory niche that was later taken by dinosaurs, until they were wiped out by an extinction event at the end of the Triassic. Many of the creatures that Saurosuchus hunted were very weird indeed—such as rhynchosaurs and dicynodonts, lizardlike animals with tusks, beaks, and short tails. They were slow-moving and easily outrun by this long-legged, agile predator.

The skull of a large Saurosuchus was up to 3 feet (1 m) long and of a similar shape to a crocodile. The teeth were large, curved backward, and serrated. Interestingly, fossilized Saurosuchus skulls contain teeth of different shapes and sizes, suggesting that they were replaced when they wore out.

The Triassic world is pretty alien to us. Besides all the bizarre creatures, the days were shorter than they are today, the Moon was closer, and the air was heavy with carbon dioxide. If transported back in time, we would not survive for long.

10 THINGS TO REMEMBER

1. All four limbs were fully erect, allowing the animal to run efficiently.

2. The skull was long and laterally compressed (narrow from top to bottom), similar to modern crocodiles.

3. A very strong, muscular neck delivered a powerful bite.

4. Teeth were curved backward and serrated.

5. Skull narrowed in front of eyes, to give a long snout.

6. Teeth were replaced when they wore out, so a living animal would have had teeth of different sizes.

7. A ridge over each eye may have helped shade the eyes.

8. Its body was covered with bony plates not attached to the skeleton (osteoderms), similar to modern crocodiles.

9. It was able to catch and kill large prey, such as this rhynchosaur.

10. Probably spent much of its time in or close to the water.

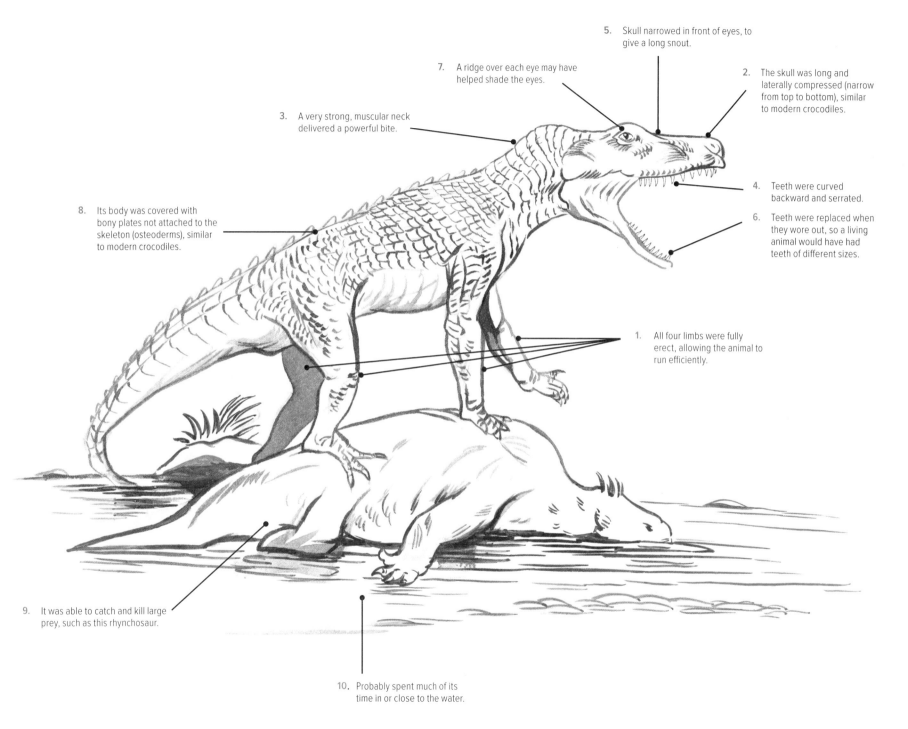

5. Skull narrowed in front of eyes, to give a long snout.

7. A ridge over each eye may have helped shade the eyes.

2. The skull was long and laterally compressed (narrow from top to bottom), similar to modern crocodiles.

3. A very strong, muscular neck delivered a powerful bite.

4. Teeth were curved backward and serrated.

8. Its body was covered with bony plates not attached to the skeleton (osteoderms), similar to modern crocodiles.

6. Teeth were replaced when they wore out, so a living animal would have had teeth of different sizes.

1. All four limbs were fully erect, allowing the animal to run efficiently.

9. It was able to catch and kill large prey, such as this rhynchosaur.

10. Probably spent much of its time in or close to the water.

Coelophysis | *Coelophysis bauri*

Late Triassic, U.S.A. (New Mexico) • 210–205 million years ago • 10 feet (3 m) long

COELOPHYSIS IS BEST KNOWN AS THE VICTIM of an unexplained disaster, lost in the mists of time. For millions of years, the aftermath of this catastrophe gradually fossilized in the Triassic sediments of New Mexico. Then one day in 1947, a paleontologist named Edwin Colbert came across a mass grave of Coelophysis, all bundled together unceremoniously. Since then, the remains of nearly 1,000 Coelophysis of mixed ages have been uncovered at the site, now called the Ghost Ranch Quarry. Nobody knows what happened to them, although a flash flood is a likely possibility. The biggest question, though, is why they were all together. Was this evidence of a predatory animal living in enormous herds? This explanation seems unlikely: how would they all find enough prey? This is one mystery that probably cannot be solved.

Coelophysis was an extremely streamlined, light-bodied carnivore of the late Triassic period. Its body form was already familiar to paleontologists from the great carnivores of later eras, with big legs, tiny arms, and a long tail. However, Coelophysis showed a few primitive traits, including extra digits its descendants later lost. It undoubtedly ate small prey, but at times it might have tackled larger meals, especially if it were actually able to hunt in packs after all.

10 THINGS TO REMEMBER

1. Its hand had four digits (three usable, one embedded within the hand). Later theropod dinosaurs had three.

2. Kinked upper jaw with sharp, projecting teeth suggests that it could have caught and held onto fish.

3. Lower jaw was loosely articulated to jaw mechanism, suggesting that it could have been moved to manipulate prey in the mouth.

4. Small, long, and light skull compared with most meat-eating dinosaurs, suggesting that it did not have a strong bite.

5. Very long legs and lightweight body suggest that Coelophysis was a fast runner.

6. It had a long, slender neck (most later relatives had thick necks).

7. It predominantly ate small prey, such as this proto-frog.

8. It had only modest claws on its hands and feet.

9. Large eyes suggest that it had eyesight to hunt and look for predators.

10. A deep belly suggests this is the robust form of Coelophysis. Others were lighter—the difference perhaps corresponding to a difference between the sexes.

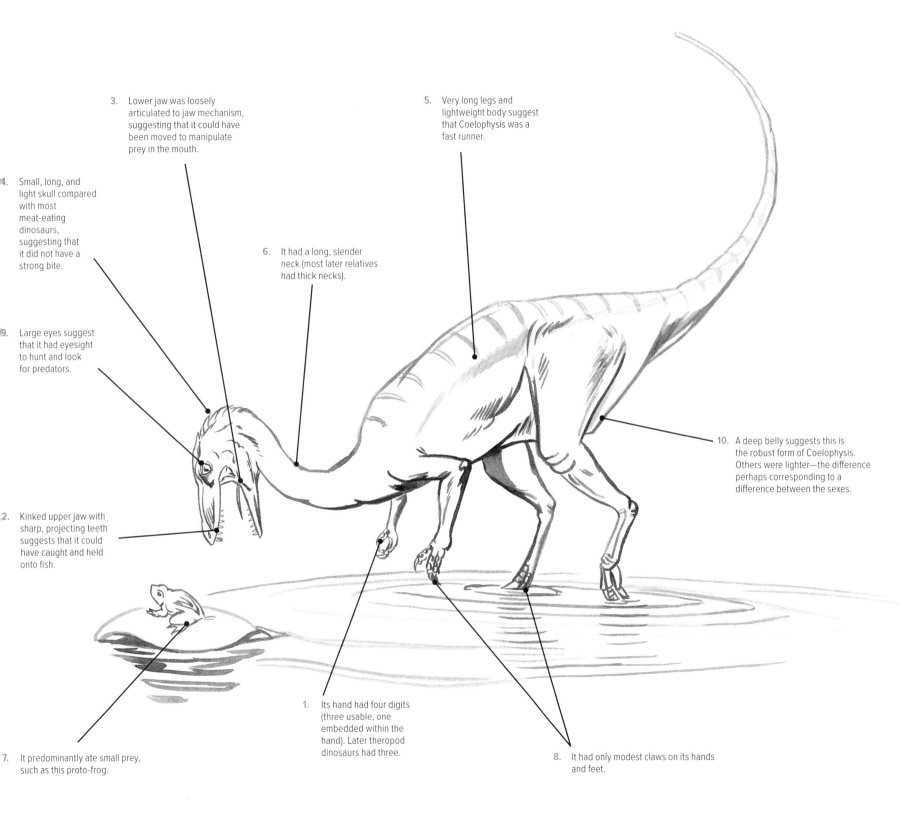

3. Lower jaw was loosely articulated to jaw mechanism, suggesting that it could have been moved to manipulate prey in the mouth.

5. Very long legs and lightweight body suggest that Coelophysis was a fast runner.

4. Small, long, and light skull compared with most meat-eating dinosaurs, suggesting that it did not have a strong bite.

6. It had a long, slender neck (most later relatives had thick necks).

9. Large eyes suggest that it had eyesight to hunt and look for predators.

2. Kinked upper jaw with sharp, projecting teeth suggests that it could have caught and held onto fish.

10. A deep belly suggests this is the robust form of Coelophysis. Others were lighter—the difference perhaps corresponding to a difference between the sexes.

7. It predominantly ate small prey, such as this proto-frog.

1. Its hand had four digits (three usable, one embedded within the hand). Later theropod dinosaurs had three.

8. It had only modest claws on its hands and feet.

Massospondylus | *Massospondylus carinatus*

Early Jurassic, Southern Africa • 208–204 million years ago • 14 feet (4.3 m) long

IS IT POSSIBLE TO FIGURE OUT THE DETAILS of family life for an animal that died out 200 million years ago? For the herbivorous prosauropod dinosaur Massospondylus, it seems that it can. In the last few years, fossil hunters in southern Africa have unearthed at least ten nests of this long-necked creature, some of which house eggs so well preserved that the embryos are still inside. These finds are especially exciting and unusual because they are 100 million years older than the discovered nests of any other dinosaurs.

One important revelation in these findings is the Massospondylus embryos. These embryos were just at the point of hatching and did not have any teeth. This suggests that, in early life, they would have been unable to fend for themselves and would have depended on their parent or parents to bring in food. That means that Massospondylus parents would have attended their nests, rather than leaving their eggs to hatch on their own—common parental behavior for most dinosaurs.

Intriguingly, the young have forelimbs and hind limbs of similar length, suggesting that they walked on four legs, while their parents were capable of balancing on two. Each Massospondylus nest contained up to 34 eggs, and the proximity of the nests suggests that the animals bred in colonies.

10 THINGS TO REMEMBER

1. It had an extremely small head with a light skull.

2. The teeth were very small.

3. A long neck was typical.

4. It may have used five-fingered hands for grasping vegetation, as well as for walking.

5. Hatchlings were born toothless, implying that adults would have had to bring them soft vegetation.

6. Hatchlings had remarkably large heads compared to adults.

7. Hatchlings were entirely quadripedal, while adults were bipedal.

8. It probably fed mainly in wet places, either in the water or beside it.

9. Large claw on thumb may have been used for defense.

10. Its body was not as bulky as in many herbivorous dinosaurs—may in fact have been omnivorous.

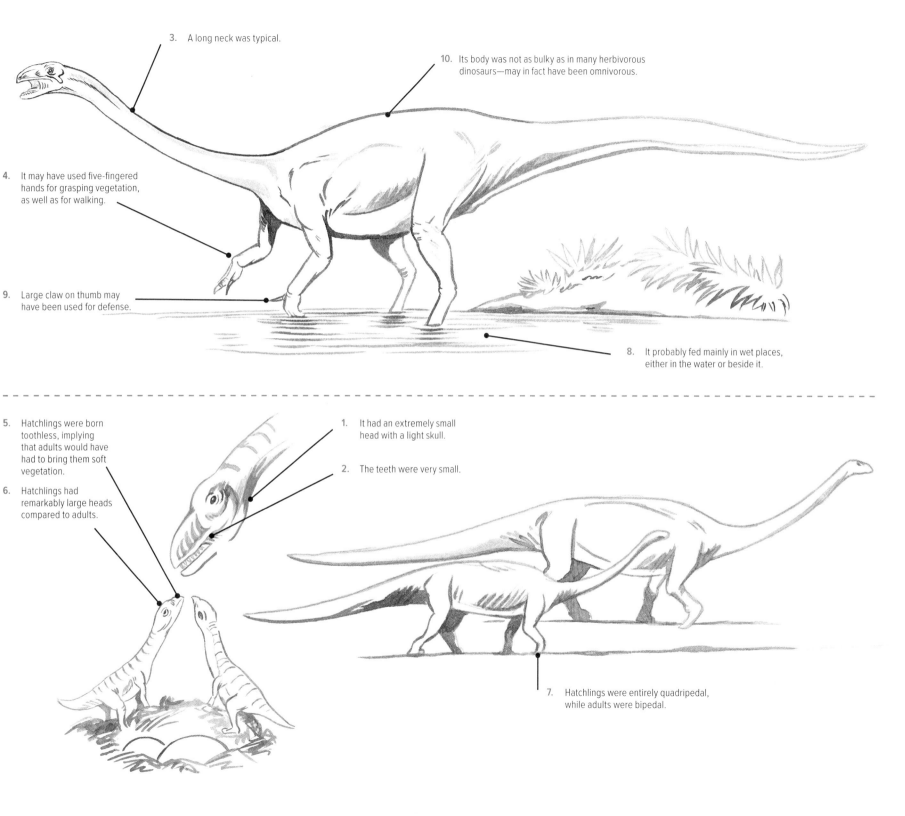

3. A long neck was typical.

10. Its body was not as bulky as in many herbivorous dinosaurs—may in fact have been omnivorous.

4. It may have used five-fingered hands for grasping vegetation, as well as for walking.

9. Large claw on thumb may have been used for defense.

8. It probably fed mainly in wet places, either in the water or beside it.

5. Hatchlings were born toothless, implying that adults would have had to bring them soft vegetation.

6. Hatchlings had remarkably large heads compared to adults.

1. It had an extremely small head with a light skull.

2. The teeth were very small.

7. Hatchlings were entirely quadripedal, while adults were bipedal.

Scelidosaurus | *Scelidosaurus harrisonii*

Early Jurassic, England • 208–204 million years ago • 12.5 feet (3.8 m) long

NO MATTER THE TIME PERIOD, every herbivore must be able to defend itself, whether it's a Jurassic dinosaur or a present-day antelope. Scelidosaurus, it seems, had several strategies. It was one of the first dinosaurs to develop bony armor to repel the bites and thrusts of large carnivores, and with its flexed arms and legs, it could run. There is also evidence that it moved in herds, another safety measure. Scelidosaurus was a relatively small herbivore, in contrast to the giants that developed later, which must have left it vulnerable to many predators.

Dinosaur biologists find Scelidosaurus fascinating because it is an obvious forerunner to the ankylosaurs. The clearest similarity is the body armor, which was simple, but extensive. The armor was embedded in the skin, like a crocodile's, and consisted mainly of cone-shaped bony plates arranged in rows, including along the top of the vertebral column. However, Scelidosaurus had longer, more flexed limbs than the columnlike legs of the ankylosaurs, making it much more mobile. It also had a narrow skull in which its small, leaf-shaped teeth could move only up and down, rather than side to side, making its chewing ability extremely limited. It is likely that bacteria in its gut helped break down its food, like the way cows do today.

10 THINGS TO REMEMBER

1. Broad hips allowed for a wide body and large gut. The large gut may have contained bacteria to break down plant food.

2. Jaws allowed only an up-and-down movement of the skull, not sideways, so this animal would not have been able to chew.

3. Teeth were small and leaf-shaped (similar to those of stegosaurs).

4. Some teeth were at the front of the upper jaw. In later herbivores, there was a beak, and all the teeth were set further back, in columns.

5. A relatively long tail may have helped with balance when running.

6. It had a three-pronged spine on the back of the skull—its function is unknown.

7. Forelimbs had five fingers with blunt claws (later herbivorous dinosaurs developed hooves).

8. It had a very small head with small brain. This animal did not need to be smart.

9. It had moderately sharp, cone-shaped armor on its tail, sides, and neck.

10. It had simple protective bony plates on other parts of its body.

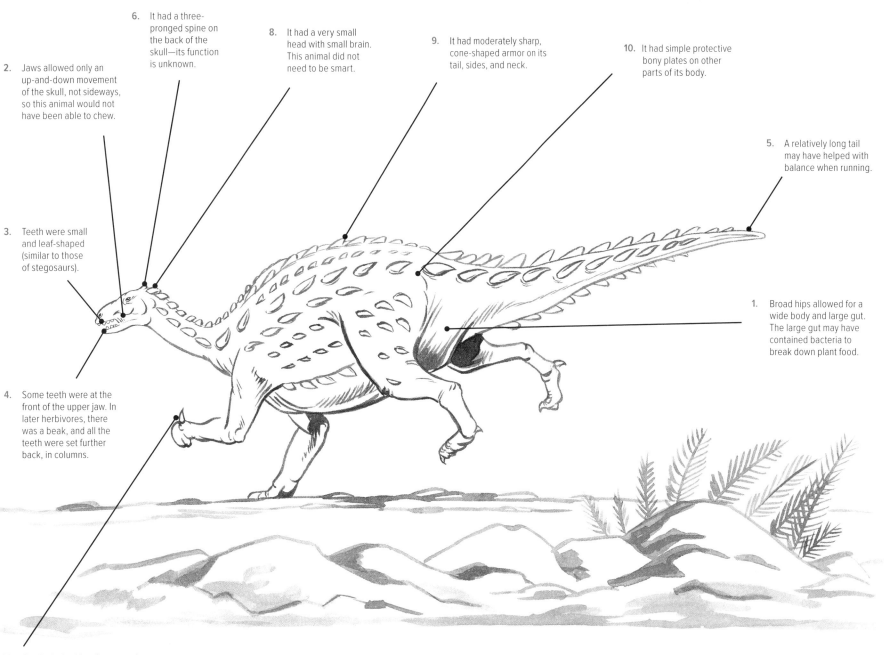

2. Jaws allowed only an up-and-down movement of the skull, not sideways, so this animal would not have been able to chew.

6. It had a three-pronged spine on the back of the skull—its function is unknown.

8. It had a very small head with small brain. This animal did not need to be smart.

9. It had moderately sharp, cone-shaped armor on its tail, sides, and neck.

10. It had simple protective bony plates on other parts of its body.

5. A relatively long tail may have helped with balance when running.

3. Teeth were small and leaf-shaped (similar to those of stegosaurs).

1. Broad hips allowed for a wide body and large gut. The large gut may have contained bacteria to break down plant food.

4. Some teeth were at the front of the upper jaw. In later herbivores, there was a beak, and all the teeth were set further back, in columns.

7. Forelimbs had five fingers with blunt claws (later herbivorous dinosaurs developed hooves).

Rhomaleosaurus | *Rhomaleosaurus cramptoni*

Early Jurassic, England • 183–175 million years ago • 23 feet (7 m) long

ALTHOUGH DINOSAURS CONQUERED THE LAND, as far as we know they never made it into the sea. However, throughout the Mesozoic period there was a profusion of marine reptiles competing to feed on the multitude of life in the water, the best known of which were the plesiosaurs. These were long-necked, air-breathing reptiles with four flippers to propel them and a long tail for steering. They probably lived their entire lives in the water, and it is believed that they gave birth to live young rather than laid eggs.

Some plesiosaurs became very large and were undoubtedly major predators. For example, Rhomaleosaurus, with its formidable teeth, thickened skull, and large size, would have been a match for anything contemporary. Aside from fish, it would have eaten squid, shellfish such as ammonites, and also other reptiles, such as ichthyosaurs.

Despite abundant fossils and more than 100 recorded species, no one knows how plesiosaurs actually swam, since no living organism has four flippers. They might have "flown" through the water, perhaps using a roughly circular motion of the limbs, but it is still unclear how they used their front and back limbs (it is possible that the front and back limbs moved alternately). Whichever method was used, these animals were probably extremely maneuverable. There were two main types of plesiosaurs: the Plesiosauroidea, with long necks and small heads, and the Pliosauroidea, with shorter necks with larger heads. Rhomaleosaurus did not quite fit the pattern, since it had both a long neck and a large head.

10 THINGS TO REMEMBER

1. It had a reinforced skull.

2. Its long teeth interlocked, suggesting that they could have been used to "sieve" the seabed mud.

3. Fish were undoubtedly a main part of its diet, but Rhomaleosaurus also ate ichthyosaurs and ammonites.

4. Forelimbs developed into flippers. Plesiosaurs had an exceptionally large number of limb digits (bones)—more than 20.

5. Hind limbs were also flippers and almost identical in shape to forelimbs.

6. Fairly short tail was probably used as a rudder.

7. Its neck pointed downward. Plesiosaurs were unable to lift their necks upward.

8. It had a large head (typical of the group Pliosauroidea).

9. Its long neck may have enabled Rhomaleosaurus to reach into seabed sediment.

10. Its short body was typical of all plesiosaurs.

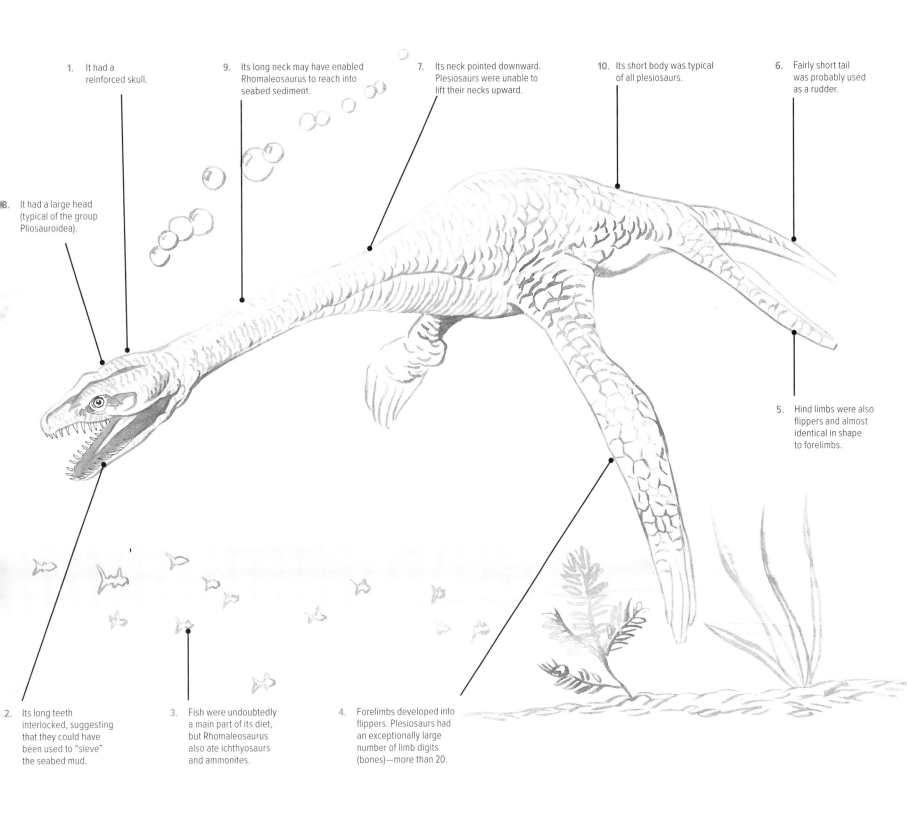

1. It had a reinforced skull.

9. Its long neck may have enabled Rhomaleosaurus to reach into seabed sediment.

7. Its neck pointed downward. Plesiosaurs were unable to lift their necks upward.

10. Its short body was typical of all plesiosaurs.

6. Fairly short tail was probably used as a rudder.

8. It had a large head (typical of the group Pliosauroidea).

5. Hind limbs were also flippers and almost identical in shape to forelimbs.

2. Its long teeth interlocked, suggesting that they could have been used to "sieve" the seabed mud.

3. Fish were undoubtedly a main part of its diet, but Rhomaleosaurus also ate ichthyosaurs and ammonites.

4. Forelimbs developed into flippers. Plesiosaurs had an exceptionally large number of limb digits (bones)—more than 20.

Gongxianosaurus | *Gongxianosaurus shibeiensis*

Early Jurassic, China • 200–176 million years ago • 36 feet (11 m) long

IF THERE IS ONE THING THAT EXCITES FOSSIL HUNTERS more than anything else, it is a find suggesting a link between groups of extinct animals. Thus, while it might not look particularly special, Gongxianosaurus is an unusual mix of two dynasties. As always with paleontology, the key is in the bones.

One of the three main dinosaur categories is the sauropods, typified by the giant long-necked, long-tailed plant eaters, such as Diplodocus. An earlier group is the prosauropods, which are smaller and have different teeth and more flexed limbs. They were the first group of dinosaurs to become extinct, by the end of the early Jurassic period. They could have been the forebears of sauropods, or perhaps constituted a parallel evolutionary pathway; no one is quite sure. Interestingly, Gongxianosaurus had a mix of characteristics of both groups—including that its hind limbs were typical of the prosauropods, while its forelimbs were typical of the sauropods. Could it suggest a pathway from one group to another? Until more bones are found, we cannot be sure.

Whichever group it was in, Gongxianosaurus shows that the sauropod lifestyle, of walking on all fours and using a long neck to browse tall vegetation, became established early in the evolutionary history of dinosaurs.

10 THINGS TO REMEMBER

1. Hind limbs were longer and more flexed than was usually found in typical sauropods.
2. Ankle articulation was typical of prosauropods (more flexible than in typical sauropods).
3. It was larger than most prosauropods.
4. Large, spoon-shaped teeth were typical of sauropods.
5. Forelimbs were long, also typical of sauropods.
6. It had a small head on a very long neck— this is the perfect adaptation to grazing on taller plants.
7. Long tail balanced the long neck.
8. It walked on all four limbs.
9. Large, bulky body indicates that it was a herbivore—plants are hard to digest, so the intestines needed to be long.
10. Base of the tail was very deep (another feature of prosauropods).

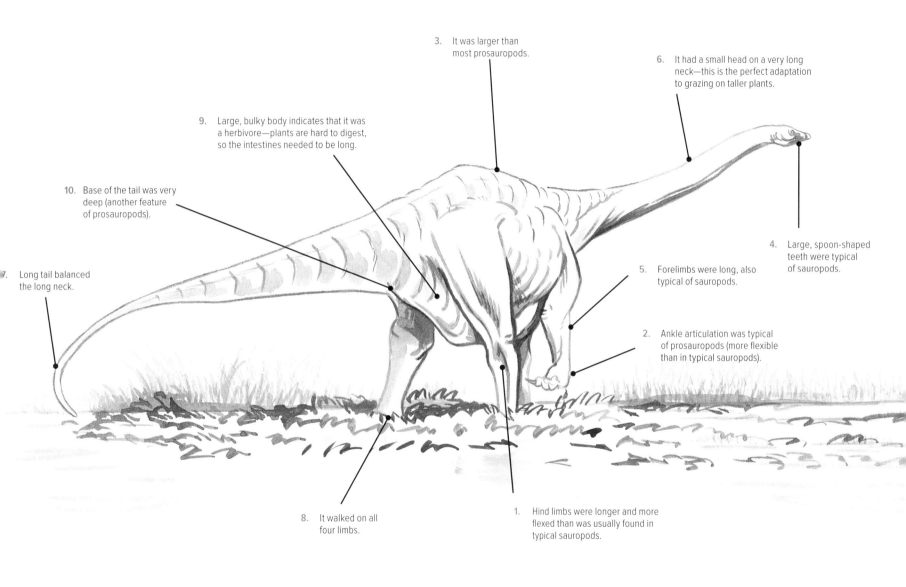

3. It was larger than most prosauropods.

6. It had a small head on a very long neck—this is the perfect adaptation to grazing on taller plants.

9. Large, bulky body indicates that it was a herbivore—plants are hard to digest, so the intestines needed to be long.

10. Base of the tail was very deep (another feature of prosauropods).

4. Large, spoon-shaped teeth were typical of sauropods.

7. Long tail balanced the long neck.

5. Forelimbs were long, also typical of sauropods.

2. Ankle articulation was typical of prosauropods (more flexible than in typical sauropods).

8. It walked on all four limbs.

1. Hind limbs were longer and more flexed than was usually found in typical sauropods.

Megalosaurus | *Megalosaurus bucklandi*

Middle Jurassic, England • 168–165 million years ago • 20 feet (6 m) long

OUR OBSESSION WITH DINOSAURS DATES BACK TO 1676, when workers unearthed a strange bone from a quarry in England that caused a good deal of confusion. It looked like a femur, but it was too big to fit any animal known on Earth. It was studied but erroneously ascribed to a giant human being. Not until 1842 was it first realized that this bone, along with others found in the intervening years, actually belonged to a large, lizardlike creature. Finally it was given a scientific name. In 1842, Megalosaurus, together with Iguanodon and Hylaeosaurus (an ankylosaur), were placed into a new group known as the "Dinosauria" by Richard Owen, the father of paleontology.

It turns out that those early finds were rare, because even today no complete specimen of Megalosaurus has been found. Nevertheless, building from fragments, it seems that it was a large-headed, large-legged, bipedal carnivore of the type exemplified by tyrannosaurs—the theropods. Its arms were relatively tiny, and its long tail acted as a counterbalance to its heavy front end. With its large, stout teeth, it was likely to have been a predator, although a scavenging lifestyle has not been ruled out.

10 THINGS TO REMEMBER

1. There were many large, long-necked, long-tailed dinosaurs (sauropods) in the Jurassic period, and these probably made up the diet of Megalosaurus.

2. It had large, stout teeth for biting or slashing prey.

3. Its large head was comparatively long.

4. It was a very massive, heavily built dinosaur.

5. Lower arm was short and stout.

6. Neck was flexible.

7. Three forward-facing toes were visible, making it a typical, if early, theropod.

8. It ran fast on its hind legs, although it probably ambushed much of its prey.

9. It had large, muscular legs.

10. Its tail gave it balance when running.

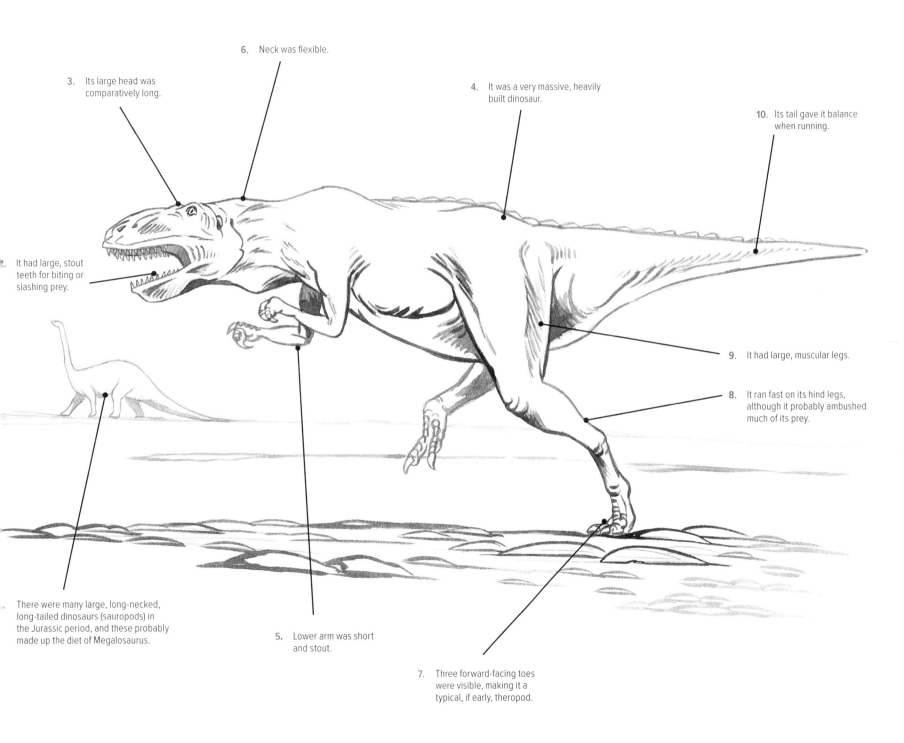

6. Neck was flexible.

3. Its large head was comparatively long.

4. It was a very massive, heavily built dinosaur.

10. Its tail gave it balance when running.

2. It had large, stout teeth for biting or slashing prey.

9. It had large, muscular legs.

8. It ran fast on its hind legs, although it probably ambushed much of its prey.

There were many large, long-necked, long-tailed dinosaurs (sauropods) in the Jurassic period, and these probably made up the diet of Megalosaurus.

5. Lower arm was short and stout.

7. Three forward-facing toes were visible, making it a typical, if early, theropod.

Mamenchisaurus | *Mamenchisaurus hochuanensis*

Late Jurassic, China • 161–156 million years ago • 69 feet (21 m) long

MANY DINOSAUR GIANTS HAVE LONG NECKS, but none match the proportions of Mamenchisaurus. Accounting for just under half the length of the entire animal, the slender neck of this Chinese fossil is the longest known for any animal that has ever existed. Its shape and size have led to all kinds of speculation, including, what was it used for? The most obvious suggestion is that this neck enabled Mamenchisaurus to reach higher than other similar animals, especially when it reared up on its hind legs—it could easily have peered into the top of a four-story building. However, another plausible theory suggests that the supremely thin neck could have been used to peer horizontally into thick groves of trees, reaching foliage that was out of reach for bulkier grazers. Another intriguing idea is that it could have stood on solid ground while munching vegetation growing by a body of water or in marshland. We will probably never know for sure.

Whatever its feeding method, Mamenchisaurus had surprisingly long legs for a giant grazing sauropod, suggesting that it might also have been unusually agile or a quick walker. Like other similar dinosaurs, it probably lived in herds and might have wandered widely in search of suitable food.

10 THINGS TO REMEMBER

1. It had an astonishingly long neck, with 19 vertebrae.

2. Its neck was unusually slender, which may have allowed the animal to reach through thick vegetation to get food.

3. Its neck could be raised high. Aside from feeding, this could have allowed the animals to display to one another, possibly during combat or courtship.

4. It frequently reared up on its hind legs to browse vegetation.

5. It had long, unusually slender legs for this type of animal.

6. Some species of Mamenchisaurus have a small club at the end of their tails, the function of which is unknown.

7. Its long tail was used as prop when the animal was rearing up.

8. It had an extremely small head.

9. Its small, peglike teeth might have been specialized for soft material.

10. It had a rounded snout.

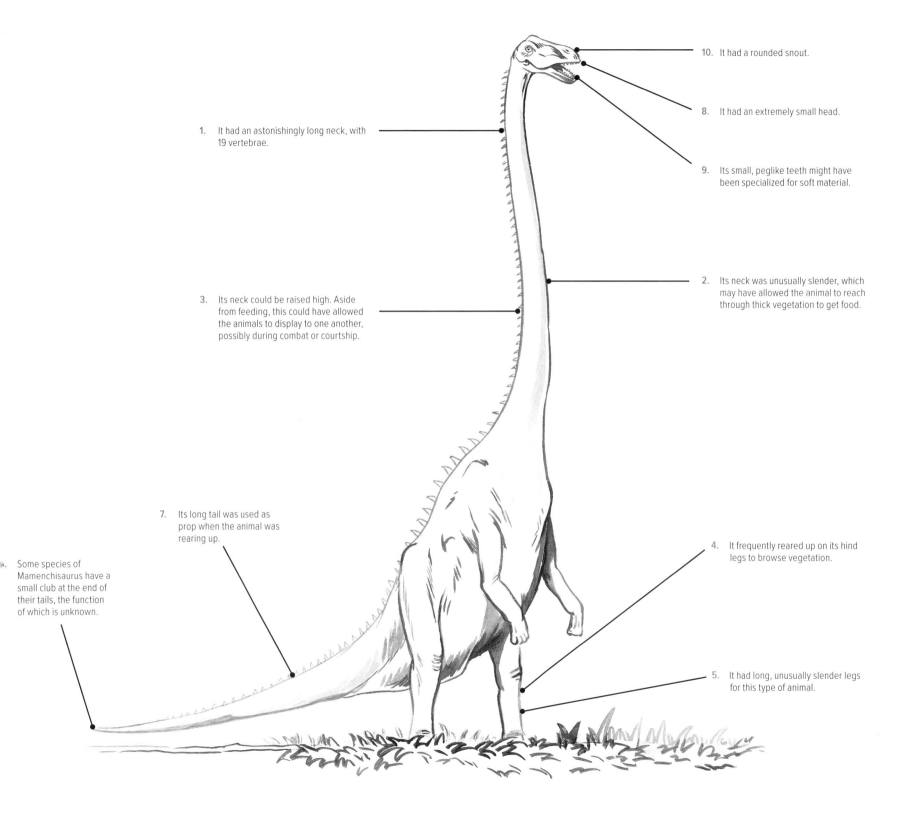

1. It had an astonishingly long neck, with 19 vertebrae.

3. Its neck could be raised high. Aside from feeding, this could have allowed the animals to display to one another, possibly during combat or courtship.

7. Its long tail was used as prop when the animal was rearing up.

6. Some species of Mamenchisaurus have a small club at the end of their tails, the function of which is unknown.

10. It had a rounded snout.

8. It had an extremely small head.

9. Its small, peglike teeth might have been specialized for soft material.

2. Its neck was unusually slender, which may have allowed the animal to reach through thick vegetation to get food.

4. It frequently reared up on its hind legs to browse vegetation.

5. It had long, unusually slender legs for this type of animal.

Huayangosaurus | *Huayangosaurus taibaii*

Late Jurassic, China • 168–161 million years ago • 13 feet (4 m) long

HUAYANGOSAURUS WAS AN IMPORTANT DINOSAUR, even if it is not a very famous one. It is an early form of stegosaur, providing clues as to how this group originated. The plates along the back and the spines at the end of the tail were typical of stegosaurs, while the flexed, relatively long legs, plus 14 teeth at the front of the jaw (later lost in stegosaurs), were both primitive characteristics. It also had some features in common with ankylosaurs, suggesting that both of these groups are closely related, with a common ancestor. The most obvious of these features is the armor-plated skull, which is broader than it is long, and a far cry from the long snouts of the stegosaurs.

An experienced paleontologist would instantly notice that Huayangosaurus was considerably smaller than Stegosaurus, and due to the fact it had little other defense, it is likely that this animal spent much of its time hiding away in dense forest as a form of protection. It was herbivorous and browsed at the lowest levels.

The plates and spines on Huayangosaurus must tell a story, but no one is exactly sure of the details. The plates along the back were much thinner and spinier than those of Stegosaurus, so the suggestion put forward that those of Stegosaurus might have been for heat regulation seems less possible for this species. And what were the long shoulder spikes for? It is possible it was a defense against an enemy striking from above—but again, no one really knows.

10 THINGS TO REMEMBER

1. Spikes at the end of the tail were undoubtedly a defensive weapon, able to inflict a lethal blow to a predator.
2. Flexed arms and legs enabled the animal to run well.
3. It had large, spikelike plates along its back. Their function is unclear: possibly defense, possibly heat regulation, and possibly a bright signaling to other dinosaurs.
4. It had a broad skull (a feature hinting at links with ankylosaurs).
5. Shoulders were almost as high as its hips (compared to Stegosaurus).
6. It had a long shoulder spike on each side, possibly to counter an attack from above.
7. It lived in dense forest.
8. The jaw had teeth at the front, a primitive feature lost in later relatives.
9. Forelimbs and hind limbs were hooved.
10. It had a moderately long tail.

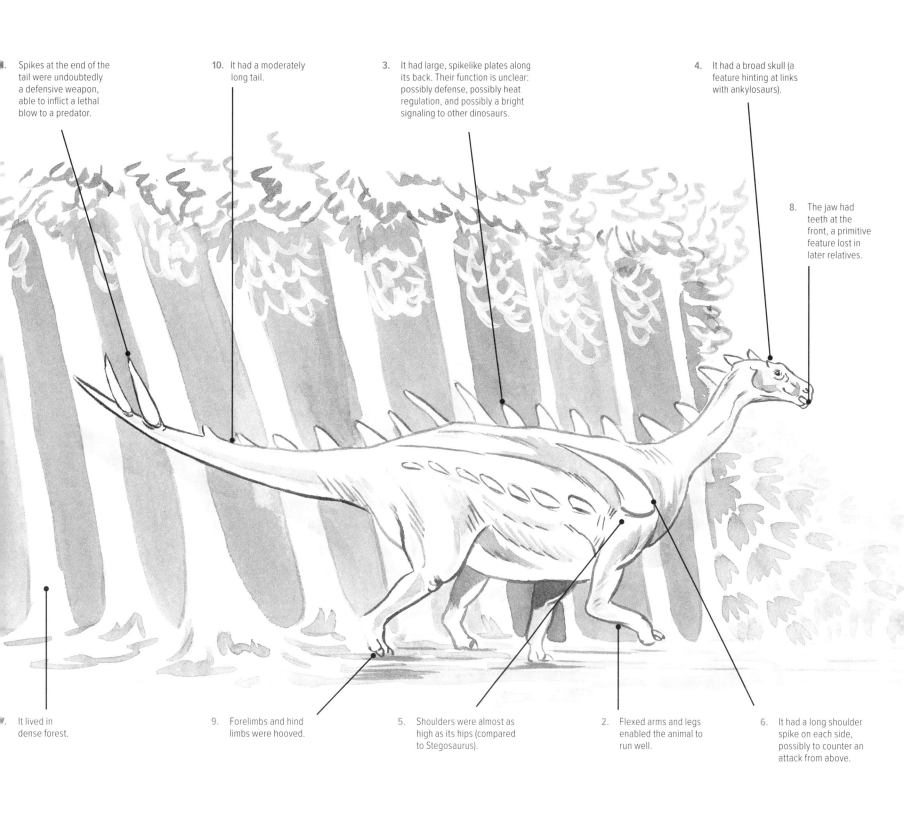

1. Spikes at the end of the tail were undoubtedly a defensive weapon, able to inflict a lethal blow to a predator.

10. It had a moderately long tail.

3. It had large, spikelike plates along its back. Their function is unclear: possibly defense, possibly heat regulation, and possibly a bright signaling to other dinosaurs.

4. It had a broad skull (a feature hinting at links with ankylosaurs).

8. The jaw had teeth at the front, a primitive feature lost in later relatives.

7. It lived in dense forest.

9. Forelimbs and hind limbs were hooved.

5. Shoulders were almost as high as its hips (compared to Stegosaurus).

2. Flexed arms and legs enabled the animal to run well.

6. It had a long shoulder spike on each side, possibly to counter an attack from above.

Stegosaurus | *Stegosaurus stenops*

Late Jurassic, U.S.A. (Colorado) • 160–155 million years ago • 21 ft (6.5 m) long

ONE OF THE MOST FAMOUS AND RECOGNIZABLE DINOSAURS, Stegosaurus was a very large herbivore. It lived during the same time and place as the formidable meat-eating Allosaurus, and battles between the two must have been incredible. We know that they did happen because some discovered Allosaurus skeletons have marks that match stabbing injuries by a Stegosaurus tail. Some Stegosaurus remains also show tail spines that have broken and then healed, the result of bashing the tail against an animal such as an Allosaurus.

This dinosaur is best known for the kite-shaped plates over the top of its back, which were arranged in two alternate rows. They were bony and hard, arose from the skin, rather than the skeleton, and were rich in blood vessels. It seems highly unlikely that their main function was defensive, since they were relatively fragile. It is possible that they were colorful and used in display or in warning, changing color in response to the mood or intentions of the animal. They might also have been used to maintain the animal's body temperature, and it is even possible that they could have moved from side to side.

Another famous feature of Stegosaurus is its small brain, a mere walnut size for an animal 21 feet (6.5 m) long. It is apparent you do not need to be too smart to be a ground-living herbivore.

10 THINGS TO REMEMBER

1. Remarkable kite-shaped plates found along back, used for display or possibly to maintain body temperature.

2. Four spikes on tail were used in defense—each was 3 feet (1 m) long.

3. There was no obvious armor elsewhere on body, which suggests that the tail spikes were its main weapon.

4. Back legs were much longer than front legs. Stegosaurus may have been able to rear up to feed.

5. Tail was flexible and used to strike enemies.

6. It had a beaklike jaw, with teeth only toward the back.

7. It had three toes on hind feet, with blunt claws (not used for defense).

8. When walking, head was only about 3 feet (1 m) above the ground. If it were not able to rear up, it would be limited to eating low-growing plants.

9. It probably had well-developed cheeks to hold food when it was chewing.

10. The jaw was small and not strong, suggesting that it might have relied on soft plant material for food.

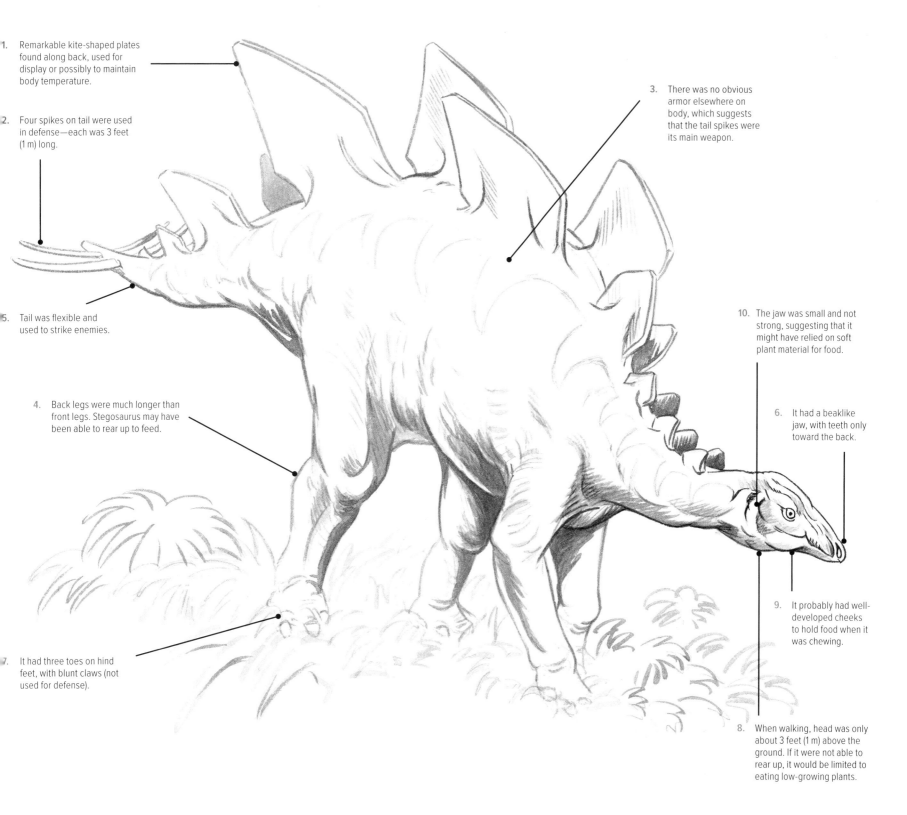

1. Remarkable kite-shaped plates found along back, used for display or possibly to maintain body temperature.

2. Four spikes on tail were used in defense—each was 3 feet (1 m) long.

3. There was no obvious armor elsewhere on body, which suggests that the tail spikes were its main weapon.

5. Tail was flexible and used to strike enemies.

10. The jaw was small and not strong, suggesting that it might have relied on soft plant material for food.

4. Back legs were much longer than front legs. Stegosaurus may have been able to rear up to feed.

6. It had a beaklike jaw, with teeth only toward the back.

9. It probably had well-developed cheeks to hold food when it was chewing.

7. It had three toes on hind feet, with blunt claws (not used for defense).

8. When walking, head was only about 3 feet (1 m) above the ground. If it were not able to rear up, it would be limited to eating low-growing plants.

Diplodocus | *Diplodocus carnegii*

Late Jurassic, U.S.A. (Wyoming) • 155–145 million years ago • 82 feet (25 m) long

AT FIRST SIGHT, THE GIGANTIC, LONG-NECKED, long-tailed, small-headed dinosaurs known as sauropods all look similar. Diplodocus, however, is of a classic, horizontal, long-at-both-ends design, with a very thin neck and tail connected to a plump body, with four straight, elephant-like legs. It is characterized by its remarkably long tail (up to 80 vertebrae in some cases), so thin at the end that it could easily have been used as a whip, either in defense or to make a threatening or territorial sound. Diplodocus walked with its neck and tail fairly level, and even today scientists argue about whether this famous dinosaur could actually raise its head very much. Currently it is thought that it could not, although it could probably rear up on its hind legs and browse tall vegetation.

One of the longest-bodied land animals ever known, Diplodocus coexisted with other sauropods of vast size, including Brachiosaurus, and these animals were undoubtedly in competition with each other. This fact makes the teeth of Diplodocus important. Completely different in structure from those of other species, the teeth that sat at the front of Diplodocus' jaw were blunt and pencil-shaped. The structure is ideal not for chewing or grazing, but for stripping foliage off branches, especially those of ferns. In this way, the animal could consume large amounts of food without needing to be too selective.

Diplodocus probably lived in herds, based on the fossilized footprints and trackways of sauropods found to suggest that the animals at least sometimes moved around together. If this is true, they would have caused considerable localized destruction to trees and forests because of the sheer scale of their consumption.

10 THINGS TO REMEMBER

1. Extraordinarily long tail would have acted as an ideal counterbalance to the neck.

2. Thin end of the tail was flexible and could potentially deliver a fatal whip to a large predator.

3. Tail and neck were held parallel to the ground when walking.

4. Teeth at the front of the jaw were ideal for stripping leaves from branches.

5. Columnar legs would not allow fast running. Diplodocus probably moved slowly.

6. It had a small head for such a large animal.

7. Long neck may have allowed it to reach in between trees to gather ferns growing there.

8. Enormous size was a deterrent against predators such as Allosaurus, a contemporary.

9. Just one digit on each limb possessed a large claw, the function of which is uncertain.

10. Nostrils opened out on the top of the head, leading some to suggest that it might have lived in water.

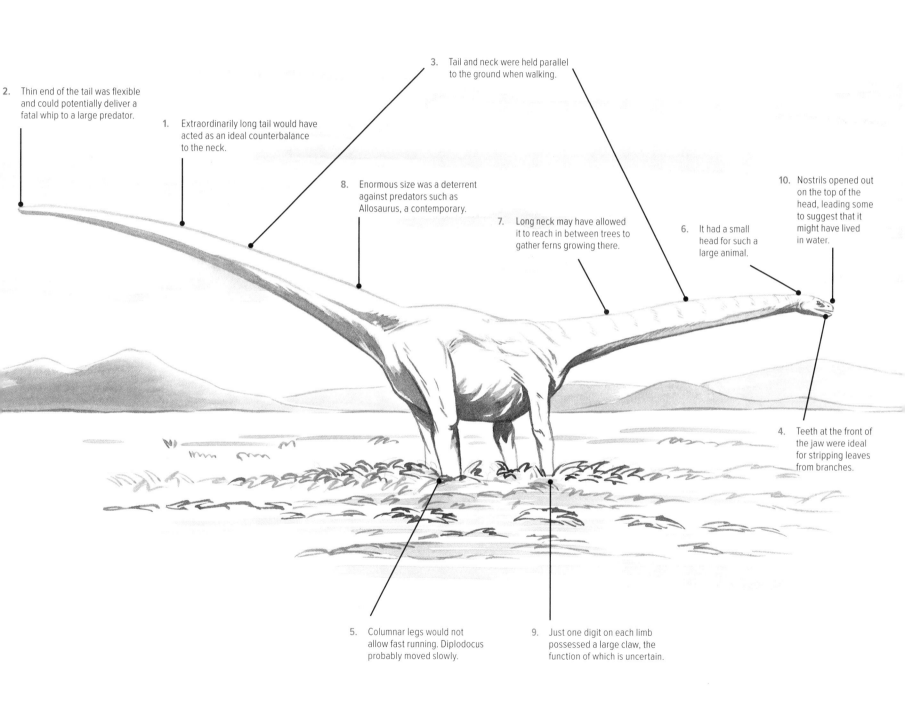

2. Thin end of the tail was flexible and could potentially deliver a fatal whip to a large predator.

1. Extraordinarily long tail would have acted as an ideal counterbalance to the neck.

3. Tail and neck were held parallel to the ground when walking.

8. Enormous size was a deterrent against predators such as Allosaurus, a contemporary.

10. Nostrils opened out on the top of the head, leading some to suggest that it might have lived in water.

7. Long neck may have allowed it to reach in between trees to gather ferns growing there.

6. It had a small head for such a large animal.

4. Teeth at the front of the jaw were ideal for stripping leaves from branches.

5. Columnar legs would not allow fast running. Diplodocus probably moved slowly.

9. Just one digit on each limb possessed a large claw, the function of which is uncertain.

Brachiosaurus | *Brachiosaurus altithorax*

Late Jurassic, U.S.A. (Colorado) • 151–145 million years ago • 82 feet (25 m) long

THE FAMILIAR SHAPE OF BRACHIOSAURUS, with its front legs longer than its back legs, is actually unique among dinosaurs, and only modern-day giraffes display anything similar. It seems obvious that the neck was held upward during normal standing and walking, and that with its head 39 to 52 feet (12 to 16 m) above ground, Brachiosaurus would easily have reached the treetops. Its teeth were also adapted to cropping vegetation.

However, the problem with these assumptions is the matter of blood supply to the head. Scientists have been puzzled for a long time as to how Brachiosaurus and other large grazing sauropods could possibly have maintained a steady flow of blood, working as it would have against gravity. They would have needed an extraordinarily large and powerful heart to have achieved this feat, and some paleontologists think that they must have held their necks horizontal instead. However, based on the structure of its skeleton, this seems unlikely in this particular species.

Brachiosaurus weighed about 39 tons (35 metric tonnes), and in order to survive, it probably spent most of every day eating. It has been estimated that Brachiosaurus ate at least 265 pounds (120 kg) of food per day and probably much more. It has been estimated that these giants had a life span of about 100 years.

10 THINGS TO REMEMBER

1. It had a shorter tail than most of its relatives.

2. Very large nostrils formed an arch above the snout. The openings were very broad, suggesting that Brachiosaurus might have had a good sense of smell.

3. Unusually, the front legs were longer than the back legs. Brachiosaurus and its relatives are the only dinosaurs to have this arrangement.

4. It had extremely high shoulders.

5. Front legs had extended pillarlike toes.

6. Long neck was probably held up like a giraffe.

7. It had a short, broad snout.

8. The teeth were small and chisel-like. They would have been used to nip foliage off branches.

9. The large bones in the trunk and neck contained some air sacs, to reduce the overall weight.

10. Hind feet had three claws, and front feet had one. Other toes had fleshy pads.

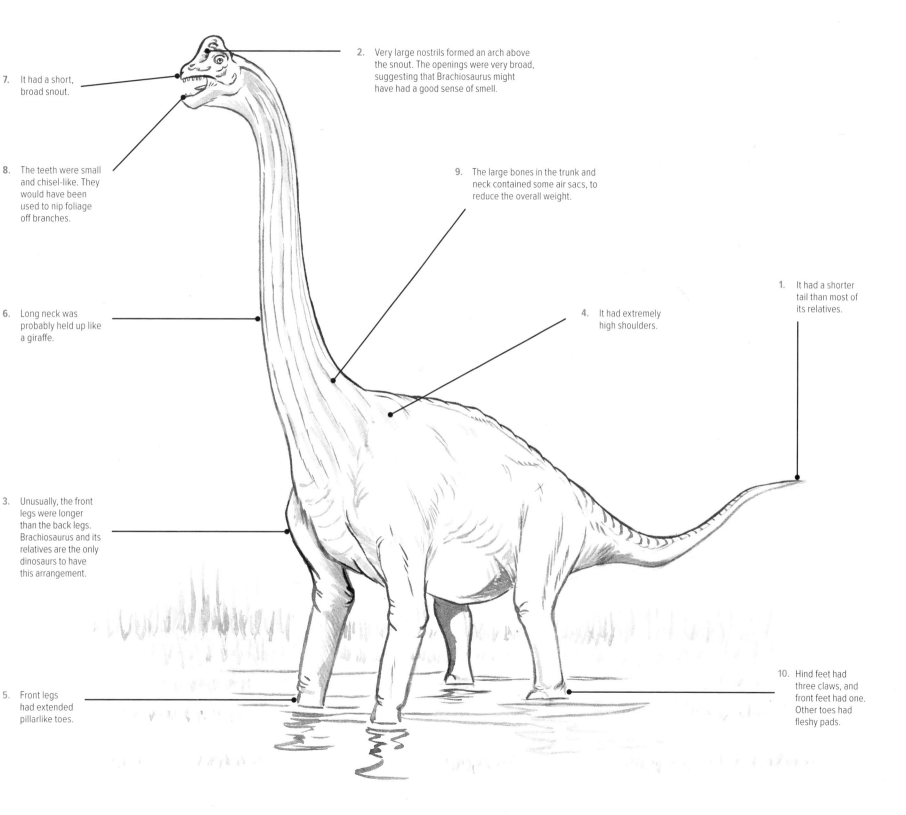

7. It had a short, broad snout.

8. The teeth were small and chisel-like. They would have been used to nip foliage off branches.

6. Long neck was probably held up like a giraffe.

3. Unusually, the front legs were longer than the back legs. Brachiosaurus and its relatives are the only dinosaurs to have this arrangement.

5. Front legs had extended pillarlike toes.

2. Very large nostrils formed an arch above the snout. The openings were very broad, suggesting that Brachiosaurus might have had a good sense of smell.

9. The large bones in the trunk and neck contained some air sacs, to reduce the overall weight.

4. It had extremely high shoulders.

1. It had a shorter tail than most of its relatives.

10. Hind feet had three claws, and front feet had one. Other toes had fleshy pads.

Kentrosaurus | *Kentrosaurus aethiopicus*

Late Jurassic, Tanzania • 153–148 million years ago • 13 feet (4 m) long

AT THE END OF THE JURASSIC PERIOD, the Stegosaurid dinosaurs were abundant, widespread, and had evolved into a number of different species. Stegosaurus itself was found in North America, Kentrosaurus in Africa, and other species have been found in China and England. It was clearly a successful group. Yet the stegosaurs would be gone by the beginning of the Cretaceous period, perhaps victims of competition from ankylosaurs, predation from the increasingly formidable theropods, or the result of a major extinction event, such as an unknown climatic disaster. They were one of the few major dinosaur lines to die out before the cataclysm 65 million years ago that marked the end of the age of dinosaurs.

While obviously related to Stegosaurus because of its armor, Kentrosaurus was much smaller, and in place of the plates along the back, it had twin rows of long, bony spines. There seems little doubt that these spines were protective, and by pointing upward, they would have been effective against large predators striking from above. The tail was also a lethal weapon; it was composed of at least 40 vertebrae and was able to flex so far as almost to reach the side of the animal, giving it a wide swing and considerable power.

A slow-moving herbivore, Kentrosaurus probably specialized in feeding on low-growing plants.

10 THINGS TO REMEMBER

1. Long spines (up to 6.5 feet/2 m long) were in twin rows along the lower back and tail.

2. Broad bony plates existed on the neck and upper back (these might have been colored for display).

3. Large spine stuck out at shoulder (presumably this was protective).

4. Its center of gravity was unusually far back, close to the tail. This suggests that Kentrosaurus could easily position its tail to strike an enemy.

5. Fairly long, heavy tail had wide sideways swing and could be used to inflict blows on a predator.

6. It had an extremely small head with a minute brain.

7. It had a small, toothless beak.

8. Its back legs were longer than its front legs, so it might have been able to rear up and browse on taller vegetation.

9. It had a broad, heavy belly, typical of herbivores with long intestines.

10. Straight, not flexed, legs suggest that it could not run fast.

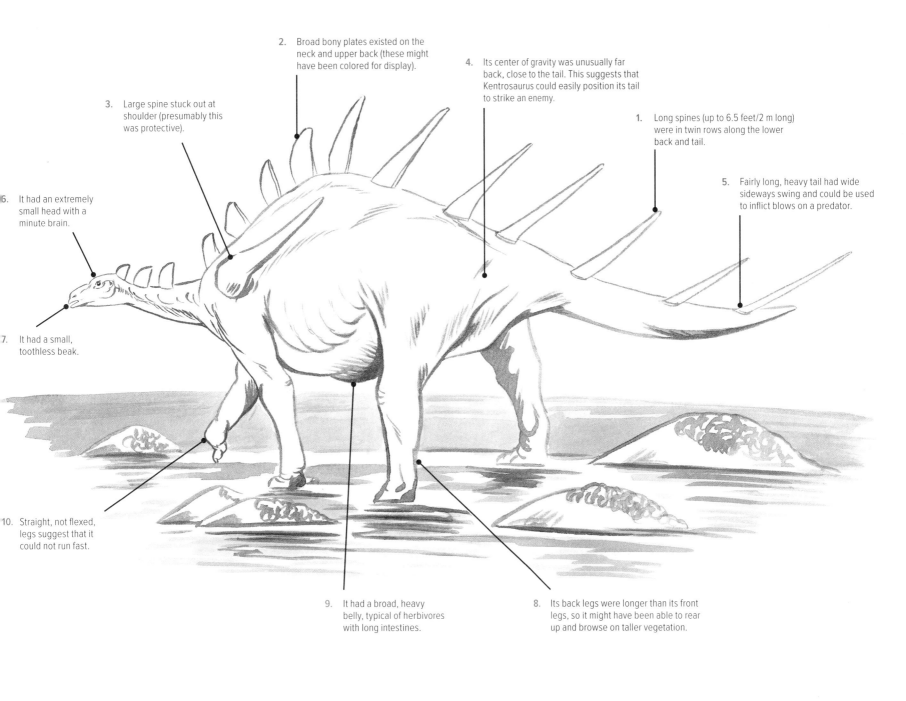

2. Broad bony plates existed on the neck and upper back (these might have been colored for display).

4. Its center of gravity was unusually far back, close to the tail. This suggests that Kentrosaurus could easily position its tail to strike an enemy.

3. Large spine stuck out at shoulder (presumably this was protective).

1. Long spines (up to 6.5 feet/2 m long) were in twin rows along the lower back and tail.

6. It had an extremely small head with a minute brain.

5. Fairly long, heavy tail had wide sideways swing and could be used to inflict blows on a predator.

7. It had a small, toothless beak.

10. Straight, not flexed, legs suggest that it could not run fast.

9. It had a broad, heavy belly, typical of herbivores with long intestines.

8. Its back legs were longer than its front legs, so it might have been able to rear up and browse on taller vegetation.

Camarasaurus | *Camarasaurus lentus*

Late Jurassic, U.S.A. (Wyoming, Colorado, Utah) • 152–148 million years ago • 49 feet (15 m) long

EXPERTS ON SAUROPODS OF THE LATE JURASSIC could easily identify Camarasaurus, despite its superficial similarity to competitors such as Diplodocus and Brachiosaurus. It was smaller, with a much shorter neck, and it also had a relatively larger head, with a distinctive box-shaped skull. Nevertheless, its presence alongside these other giants shows just how much the late Jurassic period was the heyday of the long-necked herbivores. There were dozens of species all around the world, many of them abundant like Camarasaurus. By the Cretaceous period, perhaps because of the rise of the truly giant predators, these long-necked herbivores became much less dominant.

Fossils of Camarasaurus have given us insight into the probable social life of this creature. In common with other sauropods, they lived in herds, and adults and juveniles have been found close together, suggesting that they moved around in groups of mixed ages, with the benefit that the fully grown animals could defend the smaller young. However, the eggs of Camarasaurus have been found in lines rather than nests, so it seems that the young hatched alone and joined up with herds later.

The teeth of Camarasaurus were strong and robust, suggesting that they were able to cope with tougher vegetation than their relatives. This adaptation seems to have made them highly successful.

10 THINGS TO REMEMBER

1. It had a much shorter neck than similar sauropods around at the same time (e.g., Brachiosaurus).

2. It had a larger head than most of its relatives and was boxlike in shape.

3. It had stronger teeth than its relatives, suggesting that it ate coarser vegetation.

4. A wide pelvis allowed Camarasaurus to rear up on its hind legs easily, and even to walk briefly in this position.

5. It lived in herds, probably of mixed ages and sizes.

6. Long, broad, strong tail offered defense against large predators.

7. It lived in an arid environment with localized plant growth—it probably had to travel to feed.

8. It had relatively long legs.

9. Its inner toes had sharp claws, perhaps to strike at predators.

10. The bones contained cavities to reduce weight.

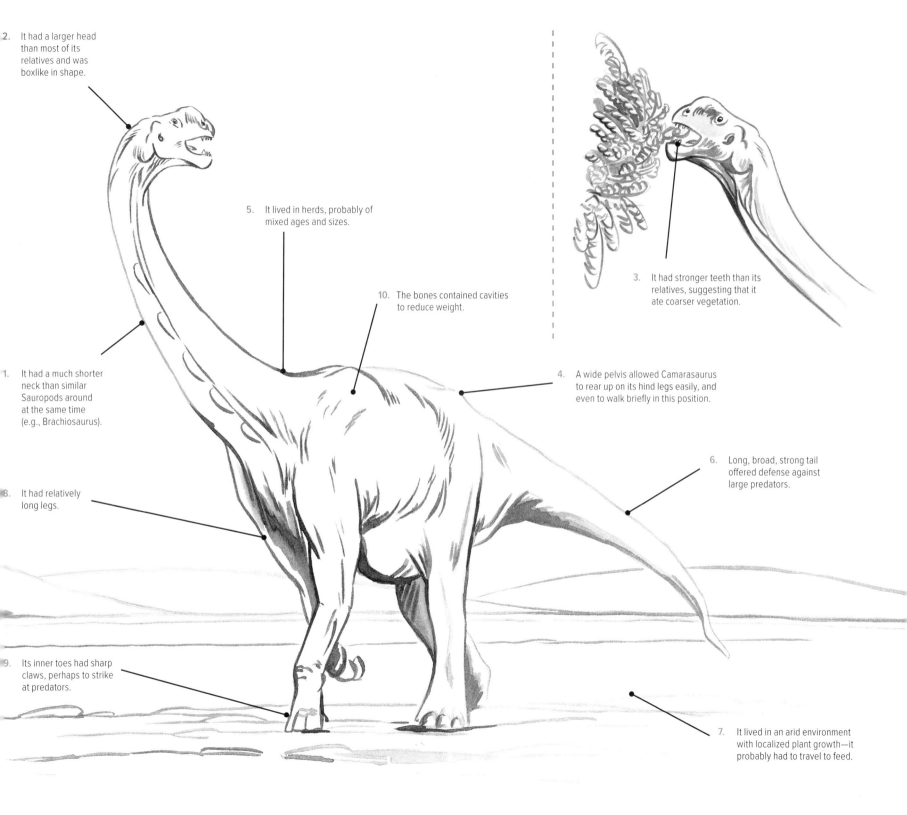

2. It had a larger head than most of its relatives and was boxlike in shape.

3. It had stronger teeth than its relatives, suggesting that it ate coarser vegetation.

5. It lived in herds, probably of mixed ages and sizes.

10. The bones contained cavities to reduce weight.

1. It had a much shorter neck than similar Sauropods around at the same time (e.g., Brachiosaurus).

4. A wide pelvis allowed Camarasaurus to rear up on its hind legs easily, and even to walk briefly in this position.

8. It had relatively long legs.

6. Long, broad, strong tail offered defense against large predators.

9. Its inner toes had sharp claws, perhaps to strike at predators.

7. It lived in an arid environment with localized plant growth—it probably had to travel to feed.

Archaeopteryx | *Archaeopteryx lithographica*

Late Jurassic, Germany • 153–151 million years ago • 1.7 feet (0.5 m) long • Wingspan 2.3 feet (0.7 m)

IT IS POSSIBLE THAT ARCHAEOPTERYX is the most famous and most important fossil ever discovered. Unearthed in 1861 in a quarry in Bavaria, its mix of reptilian and birdlike traits—including its perfectly preserved feathers—provided a significant "missing link" between the two groups. Discovered just two years after Charles Darwin published his book *On the Origin of Species*, Archaeopteryx provided evidence for the newly proposed, and controversial, theory of evolution.

To this day, Archaeopteryx remains the earliest-known bird, while also classified a dinosaur. Although the feathers on its wings and tail are asymmetrical and very similar to the flight feathers of modern birds, its reptilian features include a set of teeth within its beaklike jaws, a bony tail, claws on its wings, and a flat sternum (breastbone). The wings, however, with their distinctive furcula (wishbone), reduced digits, and feather arrangement, are very birdlike.

For such a celebrated animal, Archaeopteryx was small and rare. It probably did not even fly with much power, although it almost certainly took to the air frequently. It was an unimpressive predator that ate small prey, such as insects and possibly fish, which would have been abundant in its habitat, an archipelago of islands in a shallow sea. It might have even used its wings occasionally for swimming.

10 THINGS TO REMEMBER

1. Wings and tail were covered with feathers.
2. Flight feathers were asymmetrical—narrow in front and broad behind the central vane, just like those of modern birds.
3. Center of tail was bony.
4. Beaklike jaws were used to snatch small prey.
5. Teeth were small (a reptilian feature).
6. Wing muscles would have allowed only limited powered flight. Archaeopteryx probably glided frequently.
7. Claws on wings may have been used to grab prey or to climb within vegetation.
8. Most of its body was covered with short, downy feathers.
9. It had well-developed claws on its hind legs and probably walked a lot.
10. Studies suggest that some wing feathers (and probably other feathers) were black. This may have helped absorb heat.

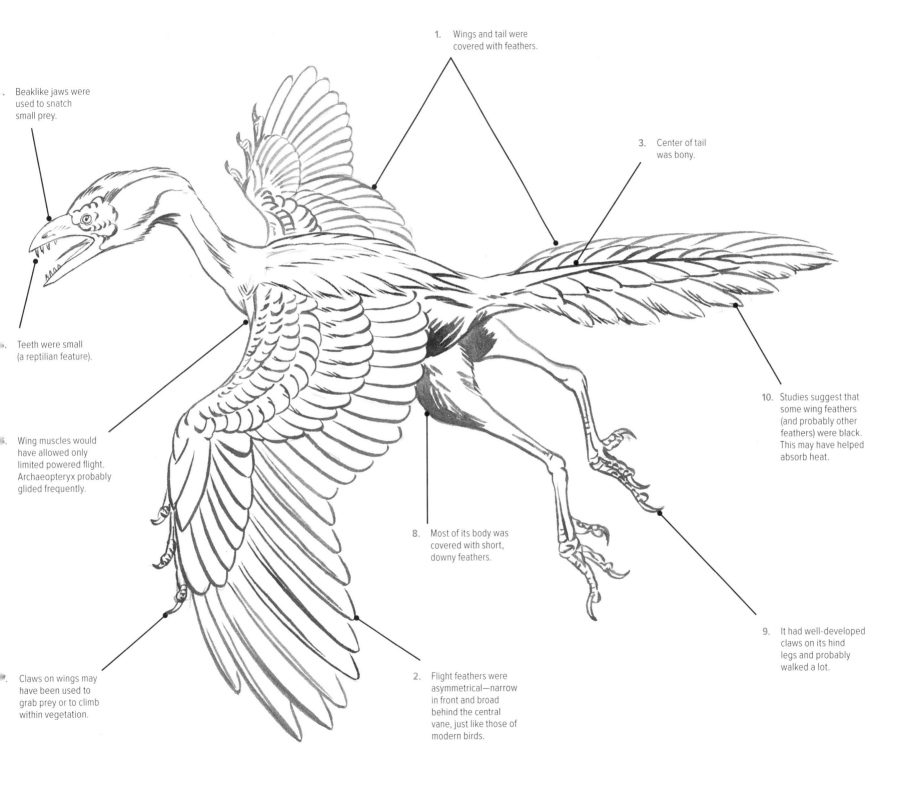

1. Wings and tail were covered with feathers.

Beaklike jaws were used to snatch small prey.

3. Center of tail was bony.

Teeth were small (a reptilian feature).

Wing muscles would have allowed only limited powered flight. Archaeopteryx probably glided frequently.

10. Studies suggest that some wing feathers (and probably other feathers) were black. This may have helped absorb heat.

8. Most of its body was covered with short, downy feathers.

9. It had well-developed claws on its hind legs and probably walked a lot.

Claws on wings may have been used to grab prey or to climb within vegetation.

2. Flight feathers were asymmetrical—narrow in front and broad behind the central vane, just like those of modern birds.

Allosaurus | *Allosaurus fragilis*

Late Jurassic, U.S.A. (Colorado, Utah) • 158–154 million years ago • 28 feet (8.5 m) long

IN SOME WAYS, ALLOSAURUS WAS the Tyrannosaurus rex of its time—a large meat-eating giant that ran on two legs. However, there are many differences between this species and its more famous relative. It was considerably smaller and had a much less massive skull, a shorter neck, and shorter legs. Its arms were considerably longer than those of Tyrannosaurus, were sharply clawed, and may have helped this hunter kill and subdue its prey. Allosaurus also had horny ridges over its eyes, shaping its face into a sort of frown.

Allosaurus was a top predator with an awesome battery of long teeth, which were serrated front and back. Some of these teeth were up to 4 inches (10 cm) long. However, recent research has suggested that its bite was considerably modest, no stronger than that of a modern-day lion. Instead, it is possible that Allosaurus might have struck larger prey with the side of its head (it had a tough skull) and its mouth open, inflicting grave wounds. In this way, large animals such as sauropods, would have bled to death before being eaten by the Allosaurus.

Allosaurus almost certainly hunted alone. Its relative lack of speed and endurance probably led to it being an ambush hunter, catching prey off guard before a short chase.

10 THINGS TO REMEMBER

1. One Allosaurus specimen was found with multiple wounds—to its feet, tail, and shoulder. Injuries like this were common among predatory dinosaurs.

2. Bony ridges over the eyes might have helped block the sun.

3. Battery of long, sharp teeth, serrated on both sides were probably used for slashing.

4. Long, sharp claws on forelimbs could also have been used to inflict wounds.

5. Arms were fairly long and could have been used for holding prey.

6. As with many similar theropods, it walked and ran bipedally. It is thought that it sometimes tripped and injured itself, as fossils show frequent fractures.

7. Long tail was used as a counterbalance when walking or running.

8. It had three main claws on each foot.

9. Strong, muscular legs were used for running.

10. Its head was relatively small compared to similar carnivorous dinosaurs.

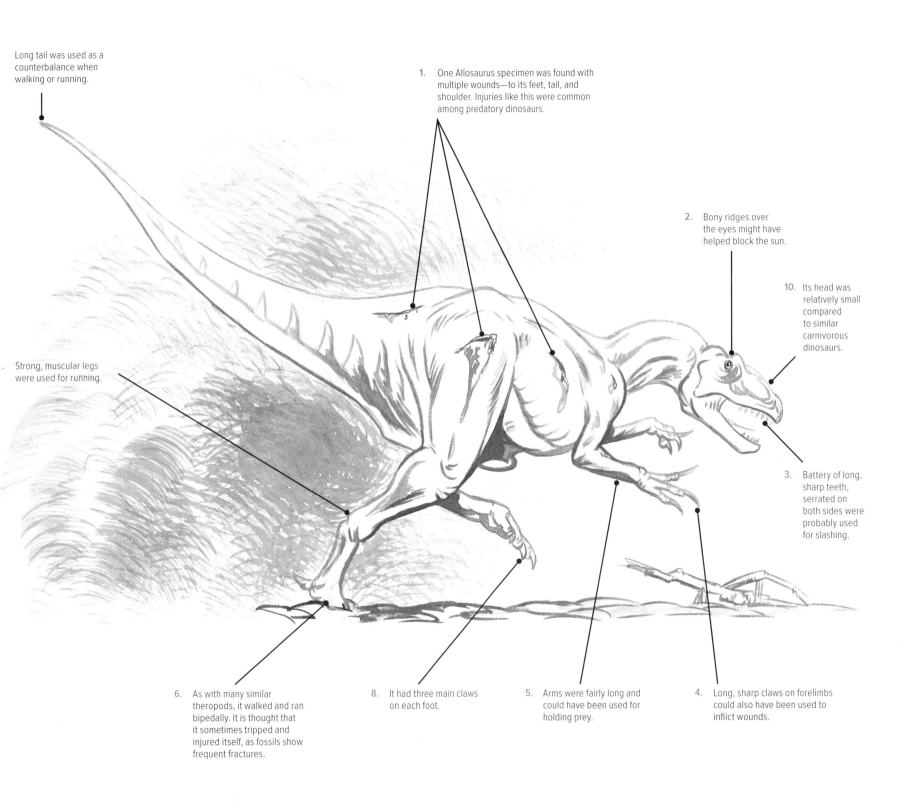

Long tail was used as a counterbalance when walking or running.

1. One Allosaurus specimen was found with multiple wounds—to its feet, tail, and shoulder. Injuries like this were common among predatory dinosaurs.

2. Bony ridges over the eyes might have helped block the sun.

10. Its head was relatively small compared to similar carnivorous dinosaurs.

Strong, muscular legs were used for running.

3. Battery of long, sharp teeth, serrated on both sides were probably used for slashing.

6. As with many similar theropods, it walked and ran bipedally. It is thought that it sometimes tripped and injured itself, as fossils show frequent fractures.

8. It had three main claws on each foot.

5. Arms were fairly long and could have been used for holding prey.

4. Long, sharp claws on forelimbs could also have been used to inflict wounds.

Iguanodon | *Iguanodon bernissartensis*

Early Cretaceous, Belgium • 130–120 million years ago • 26 feet (8 m) long

IF YOU ARE ABLE TO IMAGINE a cow that is 26 feet (8 m) long, you can get a vague image of Iguanodon and its lifestyle. Iguanodons were among the most numerous and successful of the early Cretaceous herbivores and, with their bulk, would have been prized by the predators of the time.

Iguanodon did have some defense, however. It had large thumb claws on its hands, which could have lashed out at predators. It was also an efficient runner, and experts have been able to estimate its speed from tracks and simulations as around 15 miles per hour (24 km/h). It would have escaped predators by running on two feet, but it could also move around on all fours; interestingly, the skeletons of older animals suggest that they became more quadripedal as they grew. The tail had ossified tendons along the top, which held the tail rigidly off the ground.

Iguanodon was a browser on low-growing and slightly taller vegetation. It had a long beak, enabling it to pluck leaves, fruit, and perhaps the newly evolving flowers of the Cretaceous period, and batteries of teeth at the rear of the jaw that would have been ideal for grinding food. It probably also had cheeks to keep the food in its mouth. The flexible inner digits of the forelimb might have enabled it to handle vegetation more dexterously than most other herbivores.

10 THINGS TO REMEMBER

1. Spikes on the thumb were 1 foot (30 cm) long and could have been used in defense.

2. Outer digit on hand (pinkie) was flexible and could have been used for holding or grasping.

3. Beak-tipped snout was used for cropping food. There were no teeth at the front of the jaw.

4. Middle three toes were fused together and hooved.

5. It had a long snout, perhaps for reaching plant material.

6. It had a layer of short spines along the back and tail, perhaps for defense or to break up its shape to make it less conspicuous to a predator.

7. It had the big, heavy body of an herbivore.

8. Its legs were longer than its arms, so it could walk and graze on two feet.

9. Its tail was stiffened by bony tendons to hold it off the ground.

10. It may have been patterned with dark stripes for camouflage.

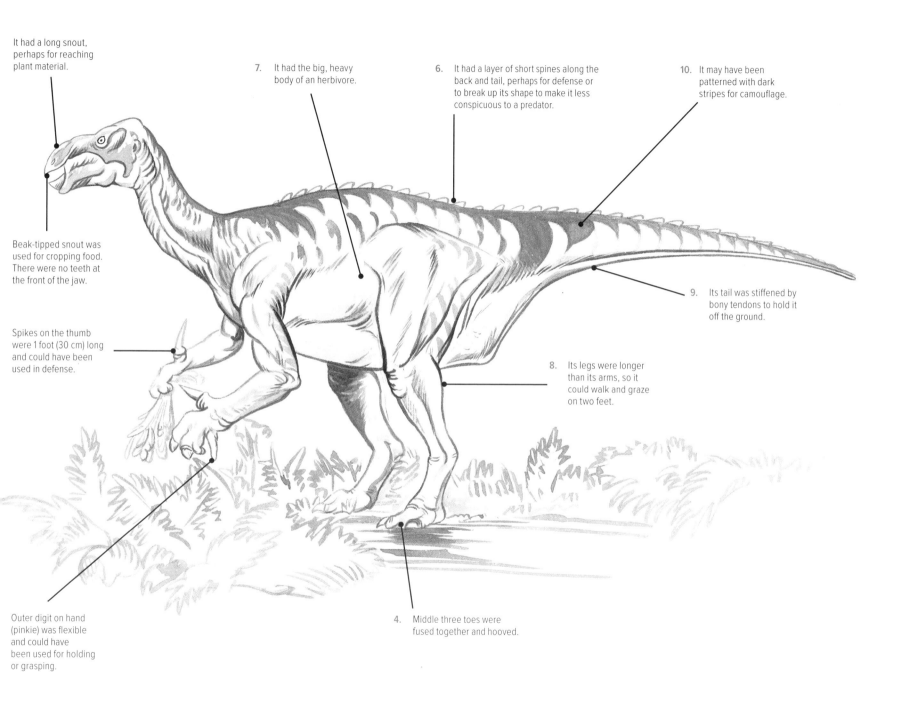

It had a long snout, perhaps for reaching plant material.

Beak-tipped snout was used for cropping food. There were no teeth at the front of the jaw.

Spikes on the thumb were 1 foot (30 cm) long and could have been used in defense.

Outer digit on hand (pinkie) was flexible and could have been used for holding or grasping.

7. It had the big, heavy body of an herbivore.

6. It had a layer of short spines along the back and tail, perhaps for defense or to break up its shape to make it less conspicuous to a predator.

10. It may have been patterned with dark stripes for camouflage.

9. Its tail was stiffened by bony tendons to hold it off the ground.

8. Its legs were longer than its arms, so it could walk and graze on two feet.

4. Middle three toes were fused together and hooved.

Ouranosaurus | *Ouranosaurus nigerensis*

Early Cretaceous, Republic of Niger (Africa) • 115–112 million years ago • 27 feet (8.3 m) long

THIS BIZARRE DINOSAUR UNEARTHED in the Sahara Desert is unmistakable, owing to the large, sail-like fin over its back and tail, which makes it look like an enormous newt. As is the case for many unusual dinosaur adornments, its purpose can only be guessed at, although it seems unlikely that the fin had any physical offensive or defensive function. Instead it could have changed color or position to make the animal look larger or to surprise a potential predator. Or, perhaps more likely, it was used to regulate the dinosaur's body temperature. It could have been turned toward the sun to absorb heat or could have dissipated heat from the surface of the skin. Another possibility is that it supported a fatty hump to store water and nutrients, such as that of today's bison or camel.

This animal was an herbivore closely related to Iguanodon, with a similar long snout, partially hooved toes, and interchangeable bipedal or quadripedal mode of locomotion. The square muzzle at the end of its snout suggests that it probably reached down to graze on very low vegetation rather than feeding higher up. Also in common with Iguanodon, it had batteries of back-set teeth ideal for grinding food. An interesting difference from Iguanodon is that Ouranosaurus lacked a long claw on its thumb; this was replaced, however, by a much shorter claw.

10 THINGS TO REMEMBER

1. It had a curious bump on top of its skull. The function is unknown, but it could have been the base of a horn used in display or communication.

2. Sail-like fin was formed by spines jutting upward from the vertebrae to make a column. The function is unknown, but it could have been for temperature regulation or the storage of fat for water and nutrients.

3. The spines were longest over the middle of the back, at up to 3 feet (1 m).

4. It had an extremely long, narrow snout with a beaklike tip.

5. Its muzzle was squared off, an adaptation for grazing on low vegetation.

6. As with Iguanodon, its battery of teeth was set far back in its jaw.

7. Middle toes of hands and feet were fused to form a hooflike structure.

8. The thumb of its forelimbs was armed with a conical spike, perhaps for defense or to open hard fruit.

9. Long arm allows it to walk on four limbs if required.

10. The fused middle digits of its hands were also an adaptation for walking, as the animals moved along effectively on its fingers.

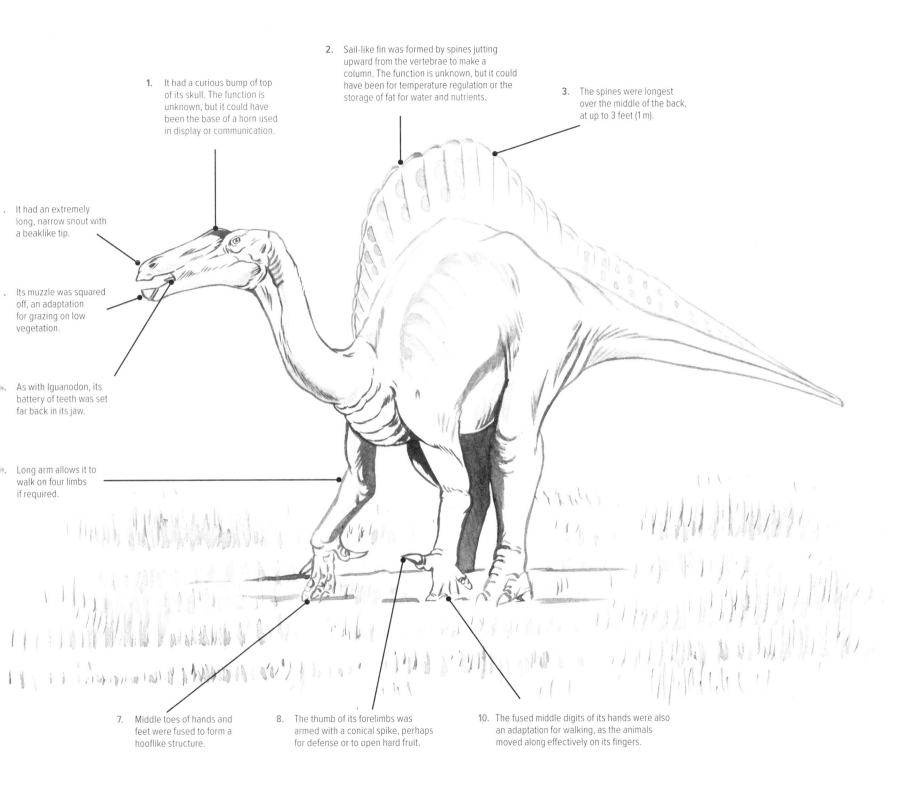

2. Sail-like fin was formed by spines jutting upward from the vertebrae to make a column. The function is unknown, but it could have been for temperature regulation or the storage of fat for water and nutrients.

1. It had a curious bump of top of its skull. The function is unknown, but it could have been the base of a horn used in display or communication.

3. The spines were longest over the middle of the back, at up to 3 feet (1 m).

. It had an extremely long, narrow snout with a beaklike tip.

. Its muzzle was squared off, an adaptation for grazing on low vegetation.

. As with Iguanodon, its battery of teeth was set far back in its jaw.

. Long arm allows it to walk on four limbs if required.

7. Middle toes of hands and feet were fused to form a hooflike structure.

8. The thumb of its forelimbs was armed with a conical spike, perhaps for defense or to open hard fruit.

10. The fused middle digits of its hands were also an adaptation for walking, as the animals moved along effectively on its fingers.

Gastonia | *Gastonia burgei*

Early Cretaceous, U.S.A. (Utah) • 130–125 million years ago • 16 feet (5 m) long

WHEN YOU HAVE THE MISFORTUNE to share your habitat and era with one of prehistory's best-armed carnivores, Utahraptor (see page 54), it pays to be well protected. Gastonia was an early ankylosaur, a group renowned for its elaborate armor, and it sported an impressive array of its own plates and spikes; the tail, in particular, with its outward-pointing spines, would have kept almost anything at bay. Gastonia also had a heavy body (2.1 tons, or 1.9 metric tonnes) and was low slung so that, once hunkered down, it would have been difficult for any predator to dislodge it without wasting precious energy.

Of course, in contrast to popular imagination, dinosaurs did not spend their entire time facing down ferocious carnivores. It is thought that individuals did battle with each other over territory or for females in the breeding season by head-butting or shoulder-butting their opponent. Such contests probably would not have done much damage to such well-protected animals, but they would have been spectacular and noisy encounters.

Gastonia was an herbivore—mostly evidenced through its bulky body. It probably fed on the lowest stratum of vegetation and, like many dinosaurs, probably swallowed stones to help break down its food.

10 THINGS TO REMEMBER

1. Gastonia may have used a shoulder-barging technique in territorial disputes.

2. Its underside was fleshy and unprotected, so the animal would have needed to crouch when attacked.

3. It had a very small head with a strong, thick skull.

4. Pairs of spines ran along its neck and shoulders.

5. Plates covered the front part of its back.

6. Rear half of its body was covered with a solid mass of small, bony projections (called ossicles).

7. The tail, with its outward-pointing spines, was its main defensive weapon.

8. Short legs meant that the animal was low to the ground. In order to kill it, a predator would probably have had to turn Gastonia over, a feat beyond most predators.

9. It had a short beak for munching vegetation.

10. It probably disappeared into a forest or brush when threatened.

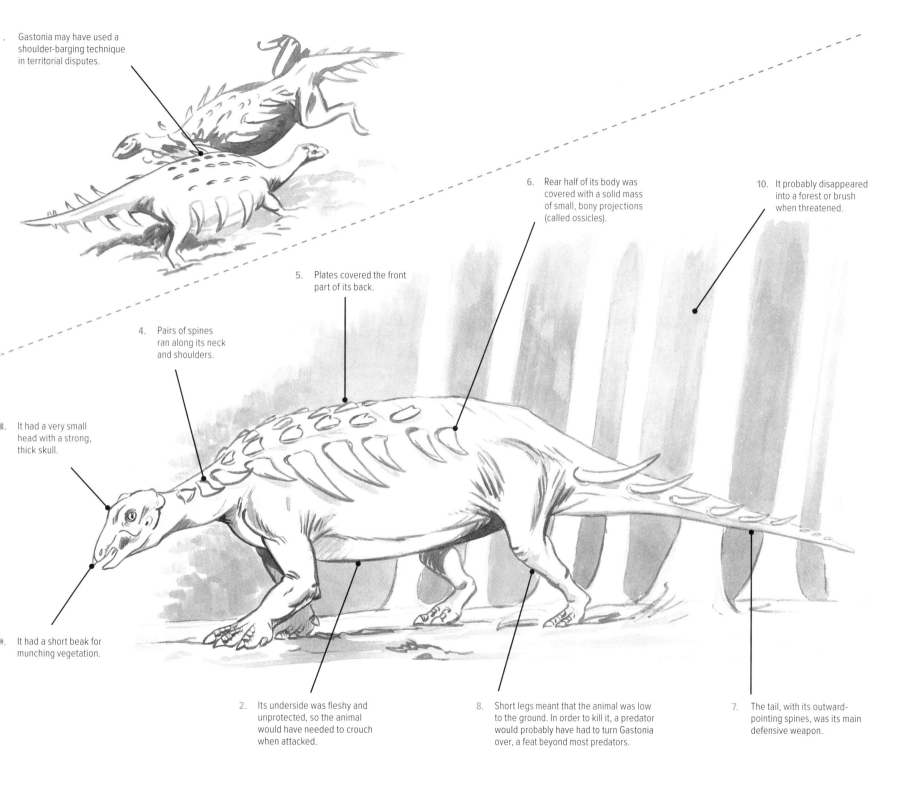

1. Gastonia may have used a shoulder-barging technique in territorial disputes.

6. Rear half of its body was covered with a solid mass of small, bony projections (called ossicles).

10. It probably disappeared into a forest or brush when threatened.

5. Plates covered the front part of its back.

4. Pairs of spines ran along its neck and shoulders.

3. It had a very small head with a strong, thick skull.

1. It had a short beak for munching vegetation.

2. Its underside was fleshy and unprotected, so the animal would have needed to crouch when attacked.

8. Short legs meant that the animal was low to the ground. In order to kill it, a predator would probably have had to turn Gastonia over, a feat beyond most predators.

7. The tail, with its outward-pointing spines, was its main defensive weapon.

Utahraptor | *Utahraptor ostrommaysi*

Early Cretaceous, U.S.A. (Utah) • 130–125 million years ago • 18 feet (5.5 m) long

EVEN THE MOST SEASONED PALEONTOLOGISTS were awestruck when Utahraptor was discovered and described in the early 1990s—few creatures have ever had such an alarming battery of offensive weapons, combined with speed and size. It seems as though this nimble-footed carnivore could have killed just about any prey it desired, from the biggest to the smallest. And the fact that it might have hunted in packs makes it even more chilling.

Utahraptor is the biggest of a group of bipedal, agile, birdlike dinosaurs known as dromaeosaurs. They were lightly built, with long legs and arms and a long tail, and many were fast runners. All animals within the species were predatory, and they were able to dispatch prey by slashing them with exceedingly sharp, sickle-shaped claws on both the arms and legs.

For its part, Utahraptor also had unusually large, strong teeth with which it could bite the flesh of its prey. The sickle claw on the Utahraptor's foot was up to 8 inches (20 cm) long. It was capable of a deadly maneuver, during which it balanced on one foot and slashed at prey with the other, using its rigid tail as support. When Utahraptor was walking or running on the ground, the sickle claw rotated upward and backward so that the animal did not damage itself.

10 THINGS TO REMEMBER

1. Large eyes gave Utahraptor excellent vision. It probably ambushed most of its prey.

2. It had large, bladelike teeth with serrations on the back edge.

3. A sickle-shaped, 8-inch (20-cm) claw on its toe was a major offensive weapon.

4. The sickle claw was on a highly movable toe so that it could be rotated backward when the animal was walking.

5. Effective use of the main sickle claw depended on Utahraptor balancing on one leg and slashing with the other.

6. A rigid tail helped the animal balance.

7. It ran on two legs—not as fast as other raptors, but it easily outran large sauropods.

8. The arms also had long claws, potentially offensive.

9. It had a larger head than its relatives.

10. It had a strong skull.

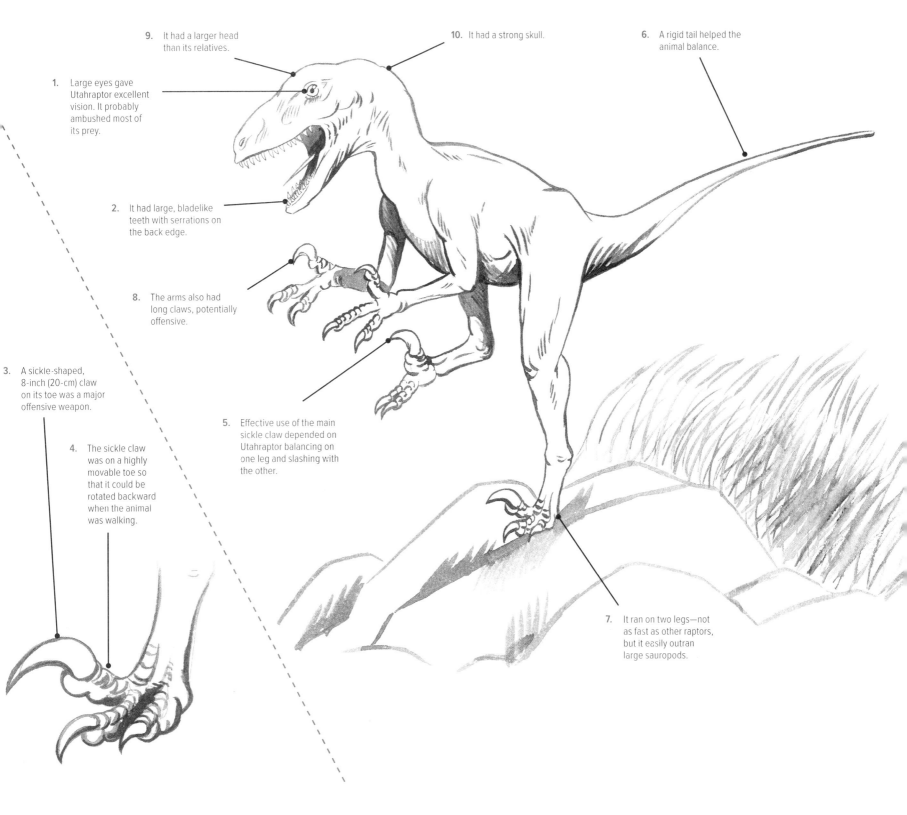

9. It had a larger head than its relatives.

10. It had a strong skull.

6. A rigid tail helped the animal balance.

1. Large eyes gave Utahraptor excellent vision. It probably ambushed most of its prey.

2. It had large, bladelike teeth with serrations on the back edge.

8. The arms also had long claws, potentially offensive.

3. A sickle-shaped, 8-inch (20-cm) claw on its toe was a major offensive weapon.

4. The sickle claw was on a highly movable toe so that it could be rotated backward when the animal was walking.

5. Effective use of the main sickle claw depended on Utahraptor balancing on one leg and slashing with the other.

7. It ran on two legs—not as fast as other raptors, but it easily outran large sauropods.

Deinonychus | *Deinonychus antirrhopus*

Early Cretaceous, U.S.A. (Montana) • 115–108 million years ago • 11 feet (3.3 m) long

YOU MIGHT NOT HAVE HEARD OF DEINONYCHUS, but the chances are that it looks familiar. That's because, under the incorrect but cooler name of Velociraptor, it was portrayed as terrorizing the cast of *Jurassic Park*. The real Velociraptor (page 80) was much smaller, just 1.7 feet (0.5 m) at the hip, and it is possible that even the kids in the movie might have kicked that raptor away. Deinonychus was a different prospect.

This was a typical raptor, lightly built and a fast runner on its hind legs. Its main weapon was undoubtedly the ferocious, curved, sicklelike claw on the inner of its hind toes, which was used to rip apart prey with a fast kicking action. With this weapon, Deinonychus was able to attack prey considerably larger than itself.

In life, scientists are not certain what Deinonychus looked like. It might have had smooth, reptilian skin like it did in *Jurassic Park*, or it might have had a full or partial covering of feathers. Several of its close relatives were undoubtedly feathered.

One aspect that *Jurassic Park* got right about this predator was its propensity to work in packs. Some fossils have been found in groups, together with an herbivore named Tenontosaurus, which would have been too large for this predator to cope with on its own.

10 THINGS TO REMEMBER

1. It had a long snout, typical of raptors.

2. It was lightly built and a fast runner. Tracks attributed to Deinonychus have been used to estimate its speed at 6 miles per hour (10.1 km/h).

3. There were about 70 sharp, curved teeth in its jaw. The bite has been estimated as having been as powerful as a hyena's.

4. The skin may actually have been covered with primitive feathers.

5. It had three digits with sharp claws on its forelimbs.

6. The arms of juveniles were proportionally longer than those of adults, so perhaps they had slightly different methods of hunting.

7. It had a very long (and sharp) inner claw of both feet. It was usually sickle-shaped, but varied between individuals.

8. The tail is moderately long and may have been able to swing from side to side.

9. Palms of the hands face inward, enabling it to clutch its prey.

10. Light shape and fleet-footed nature suggests that it was warm-blooded (endothermic).

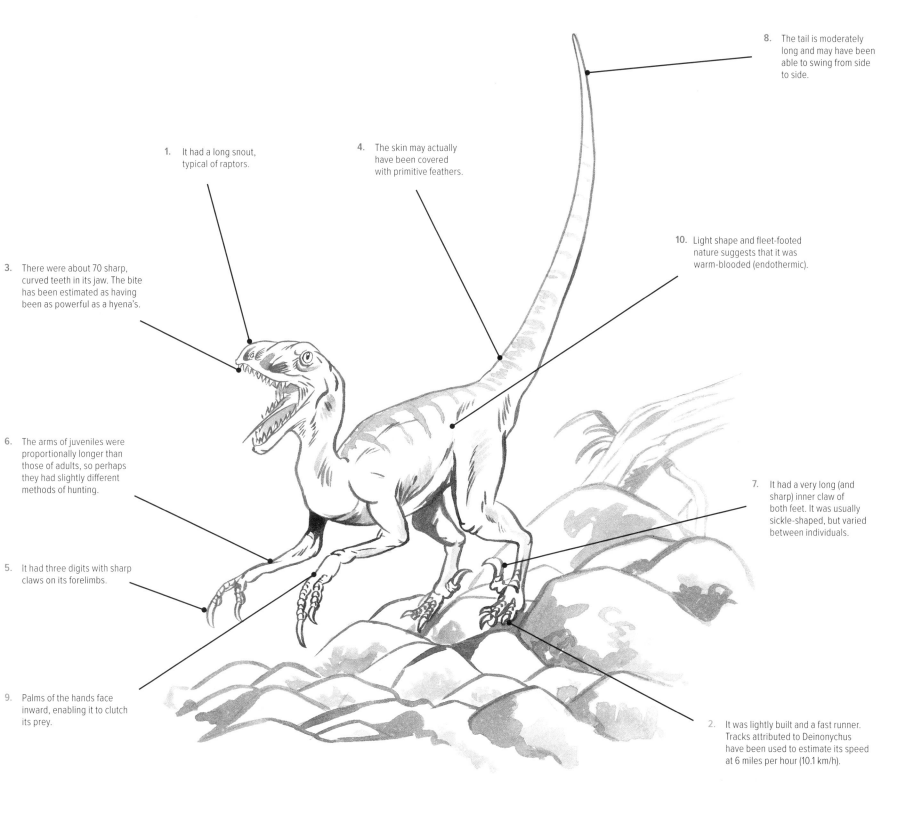

8. The tail is moderately long and may have been able to swing from side to side.

1. It had a long snout, typical of raptors.

4. The skin may actually have been covered with primitive feathers.

10. Light shape and fleet-footed nature suggests that it was warm-blooded (endothermic).

3. There were about 70 sharp, curved teeth in its jaw. The bite has been estimated as having been as powerful as a hyena's.

6. The arms of juveniles were proportionally longer than those of adults, so perhaps they had slightly different methods of hunting.

7. It had a very long (and sharp) inner claw of both feet. It was usually sickle-shaped, but varied between individuals.

5. It had three digits with sharp claws on its forelimbs.

9. Palms of the hands face inward, enabling it to clutch its prey.

2. It was lightly built and a fast runner. Tracks attributed to Deinonychus have been used to estimate its speed at 6 miles per hour (10.1 km/h).

Microraptor | *Microraptor zhaoianus*

Early Cretaceous, China • 125–115 million years ago • 2.3 feet (0.7 m) • Wingspan 2.5 feet (0.75 m)

DINOSAURS EVOLVED SOME STRANGE FORMS, but very few would have looked quite as alien to us as Microraptor. Imagine wandering through the early Cretaceous forests and seeing a birdlike creature gliding above you on four—yes, four!—separate wings. All of Microraptor's limbs were fully feathered, including a long tail with a diamond-shaped tip. Bizarrely, the feathers on its hind wings reached right down to the top of its foot.

Despite all these aerial appendages, it is by no means certain that Microraptor could fly very well, if at all. It is unlikely that it could have taken off from the ground, so it probably simply glided from tree to tree. The rest of its body was also covered in feathers, and recent research has revealed that most of these feathers were glossy black, like those of many modern birds.

Some Microraptor fossils are so well preserved that some of their gut contents can be analyzed, a very rare example of direct evidence of diet. It seems that Microraptor ate small vertebrates, including small mammals; recently bird bones have also been found. The likelihood is that it had a broad diet.

10 THINGS TO REMEMBER

1. It was very small for a dinosaur, no bigger than a gull.

2. A full set of asymmetrical flight feathers were attached to the forewings, similar to those of modern birds.

3. Legs were very long and supported the second wing of asymmetrical feathers extending to the foot.

4. The tail was long and feathered.

5. Short feathers also covered most of the body.

6. Small teeth with modest serrations suggest that Microraptor ate small prey.

7. Long wings would have dragged along the ground when Microraptor tried to walk, suggesting that it was probably arboreal.

8. Small feather crest was probably used to signal to other members of the species.

9. Its main color was glossy black.

10. It had a small, light body.

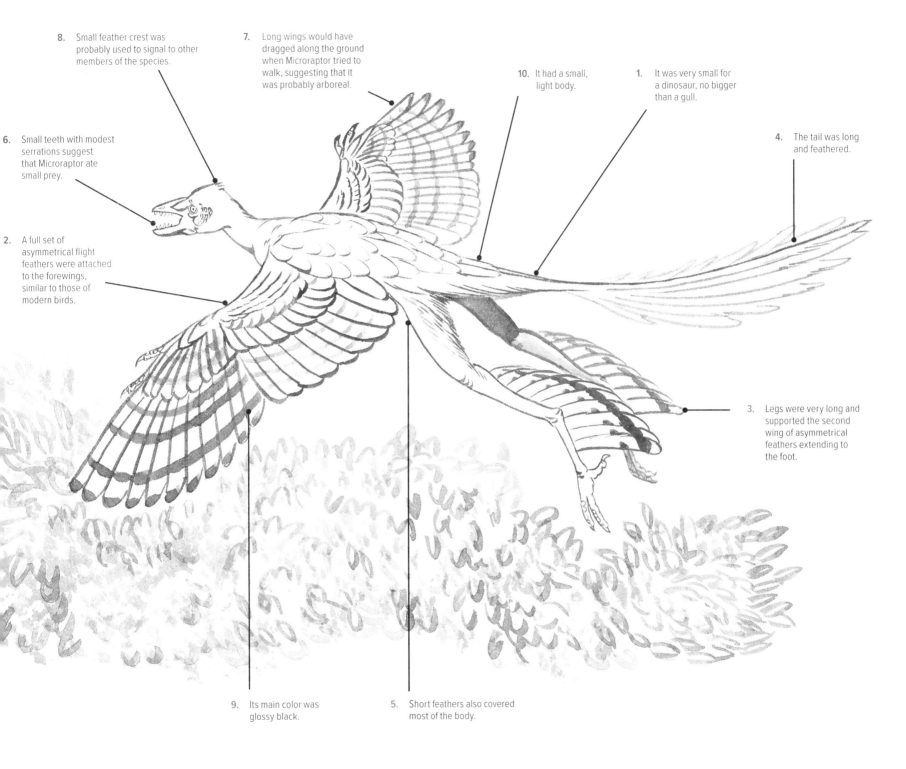

8. Small feather crest was probably used to signal to other members of the species.

7. Long wings would have dragged along the ground when Microraptor tried to walk, suggesting that it was probably arboreal.

10. It had a small, light body.

1. It was very small for a dinosaur, no bigger than a gull.

4. The tail was long and feathered.

6. Small teeth with modest serrations suggest that Microraptor ate small prey.

2. A full set of asymmetrical flight feathers were attached to the forewings, similar to those of modern birds.

3. Legs were very long and supported the second wing of asymmetrical feathers extending to the foot.

9. Its main color was glossy black.

5. Short feathers also covered most of the body.

Sinosauropteryx | *Sinosauropteryx prima*

Early Cretaceous, China • 125–120 million years ago • 3 feet (1 m) long

THIS IS ONE OF THE FEW DINOSAURS in this book whose coloring we know for sure. Microscopic studies on fossil feathers of Sinosauropteryx have enabled scientists to study the structure of melanosomes, the cells that give feathers their color. They reveal that the tail of this animal had alternating dark and pale bands. It is thought that the dark tail bands were reddish-brown and that a chestnut coloration appeared on the upperside of the rest of the animal.

When first uncovered in 1996, Sinosauropteryx caused a storm of controversy because of the filaments that copiously covered its body. The suggestion that the filaments were primitive proto-feathers had all kinds of implications, breaking down all pretense of a boundary between dinosaurs, which Sinosauropteryx clearly was, and birds. These days it is generally accepted that this animal was the first nonavian dinosaur to be discovered with feathers, albeit very small ones that were used for insulation rather than for flying. The feathery cloak was strong evidence that Sinosauropteryx was warm-blooded, quick moving, and active. In recent years we have come a long way from the notion that dinosaurs were slow, lumbering, or even extinct. Today, we know they live on as modern birds.

Sinosauropteryx was a predator that ran after its prey. Recent analysis of the remarkable fossils from Liaoning, China, has unveiled a small lizard inside the gut of one, and a couple of small mammals inside of another.

10 THINGS TO REMEMBER

1. It had an extremely long, slender tail with 64 vertebrae.

2. Its tail showed bands of alternating dark reddish-brown and a pale color, perhaps to disrupt the shape of the animal or to draw attention away from the vulnerable parts of its body.

3. The thick covering of filaments, especially along its back, were presumably for insulation. Some filaments were 1 inch (30 cm) long.

4. Its long legs were used for running along the ground and leaping.

5. It had rather short arms, similar to a mini version of its relative, the T. rex.

6. Large thumb claws may have been used in hunting and possibly during combat between individuals.

7. It had a long snout with good reach.

8. It had small teeth, indicating that these were not its main weapons.

9. Insects such as dragonflies would have doubtless constituted some of its prey, but lizards and mammals have also been found in preserved intestines.

10. Filaments gave a "fuzzy" look to its body.

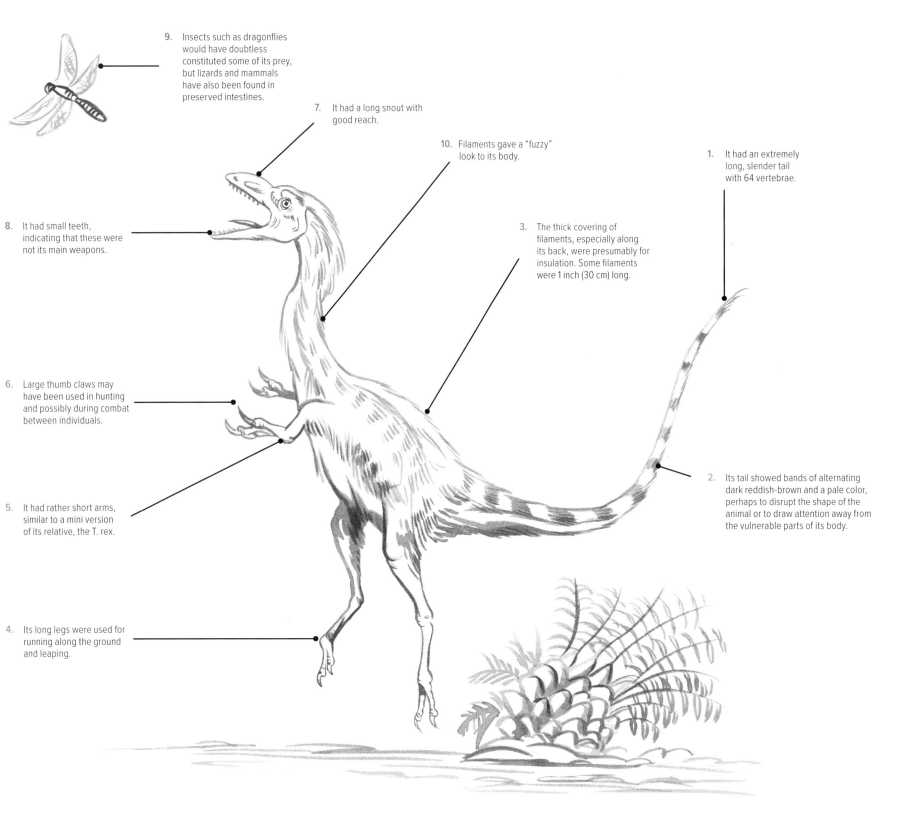

9. Insects such as dragonflies would have doubtless constituted some of its prey, but lizards and mammals have also been found in preserved intestines.

7. It had a long snout with good reach.

10. Filaments gave a "fuzzy" look to its body.

1. It had an extremely long, slender tail with 64 vertebrae.

8. It had small teeth, indicating that these were not its main weapons.

3. The thick covering of filaments, especially along its back, were presumably for insulation. Some filaments were 1 inch (30 cm) long.

6. Large thumb claws may have been used in hunting and possibly during combat between individuals.

2. Its tail showed bands of alternating dark reddish-brown and a pale color, perhaps to disrupt the shape of the animal or to draw attention away from the vulnerable parts of its body.

5. It had rather short arms, similar to a mini version of its relative, the T. rex.

4. Its long legs were used for running along the ground and leaping.

Tupandactylus | *Tupandactylus imperator*

Early Cretaceous, Brazil • 112 million years ago • Wingspan 8 feet (2.5 m)

HAD PREHISTORIC TOURISM EVER EXISTED, one destination of choice would have been northern Brazil in the early Cretaceous period. There, the skies were home to some of the most spectacular pterosaurs the world had ever known, with seven species of bizarre forms bearing bright crests, outsize beaks, and probably diverse feeding behavior. One of the most spectacular was Tupandactylus, a moderate-size pterosaur with simply astonishing head adornments.

The skull of Tupandactylus was 2.5 feet (76 cm) long from front to back, with a huge crest that, on speculation, was brightly colored—after all, the crest was unlikely to have any function other than as an advertisement to other members of the species. Aside from a bony rod on the front and top, and a similarly bony rod projecting behind it, most of the crest was made up of soft tissue such as keratin. There was also a keratin beak, which was short for a pterosaur, while the lower jaw had a curious "keel" projecting downward, for reasons that remain unknown.

Since Tupandactylus remains were found on sediments next to a large inland sea, it seems reasonable to assume that these dinosaurs ate fish. However, the short beak would not have been ideal for catching fish in water; it was more suited to scavenging dead or stranded ones. Another, more imaginative suggestion is that it might have plucked fruit instead and not eaten fish at all.

10 THINGS TO REMEMBER

1. It had no teeth, typical of a later pterosaur.
2. Its beak was short and fairly broad, suggesting a scavenging, or possibly fruit, diet.
3. It had an enormous head crest, probably for ornamentation, although it might have had some kind of aerodynamic property.
4. The crest would probably have been brightly colored, to signal to other individuals.
5. It had a large nasal opening in front of its eyes. It is possible that its sense of smell was highly developed.
6. Large eyes (and features of the brain) suggest that these pterosaurs had excellent vision.
7. Its wings were set slightly farther forward than in some pterosaurs.
8. The wings, as in other pterosaurs, were formed by large leathery flaps of skin that were held in place by vastly extended fourth digits on the hands.
9. Forward membrane (protopagium) was held in place by a bone unique to pterosaurs.
10. The short tail connected to the legs with a flap of skin.

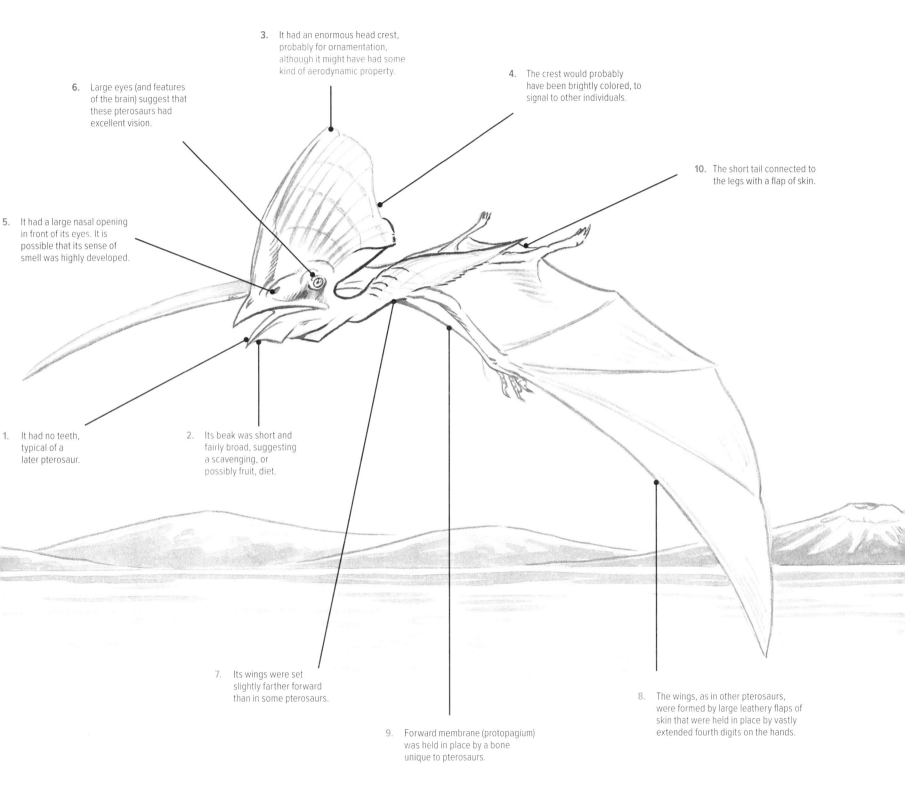

3. It had an enormous head crest, probably for ornamentation, although it might have had some kind of aerodynamic property.

6. Large eyes (and features of the brain) suggest that these pterosaurs had excellent vision.

4. The crest would probably have been brightly colored, to signal to other individuals.

10. The short tail connected to the legs with a flap of skin.

5. It had a large nasal opening in front of its eyes. It is possible that its sense of smell was highly developed.

1. It had no teeth, typical of a later pterosaur.

2. Its beak was short and fairly broad, suggesting a scavenging, or possibly fruit, diet.

7. Its wings were set slightly farther forward than in some pterosaurs.

9. Forward membrane (protopagium) was held in place by a bone unique to pterosaurs.

8. The wings, as in other pterosaurs, were formed by large leathery flaps of skin that were held in place by vastly extended fourth digits on the hands.

Amargasaurus | *Amargasaurus cazaui*

Early Cretaceous, Argentina • 131–125 million years ago • 43 feet (13 m) long

IN CASE YOU THOUGHT THAT ALL THE MIGHTY, long-necked, herbivorous sauropods looked similar, here's a notable exception. Known from just a single skeleton found in Argentina, Amargasaurus is unusual in a number of ways. Not only does it have an exceptionally short neck, which must have limited the height at which it could feed, but that neck was covered with a double row of very long spines, which makes the skeleton look as though it had a mane. Unless more remains are found, we will never know what this strange dinosaur actually looked like in life, nor do we know the mane's purpose.

There are theories, of course. One is that the spines supported a sail-like fin, similar to that seen in other dinosaurs such as the Spinosaurus. If so, it could have been used for temperature regulation or for signaling to other individuals. In fact, there is also a smaller section of single spines along the back of Amargasaurus, lending some weight to this idea. Equally, the bones on the neck could have been separate, as in the illustration, and used in some form of defense. One particularly interesting suggestion is that the animal could have clattered these bones together to make a loud, threatening sound.

One thing that the "mane" did do was restrict the height to which the neck could be raised. This confirms that Amargasaurus probably ate plants only at a moderate height above ground.

10 THINGS TO REMEMBER

1. It had a long neck typical of sauropods, but much shorter than many similar species.

2. It had an extremely long tail, possibly with a whiplike tip.

3. The neck had extraordinary long spines, the function of which partly depends on whether they supported a sail or were separate. If the latter, they could have been used in defense.

4. Smaller spines on the back probably supported a sail-like fin.

5. Neck spines could have clattered together to make a noise to scare an enemy or intimidate a rival.

6. It had plodding feet with five toes in a hooflike arrangement.

7. Its large body suggested a vegetarian diet. The look of its skull and teeth is unknown.

8. Its habitat was forests with abundant water.

9. It had short, nonoverlapping ribs that allowed for extra movement of the neck.

10. Its back legs were slightly longer than its front legs.

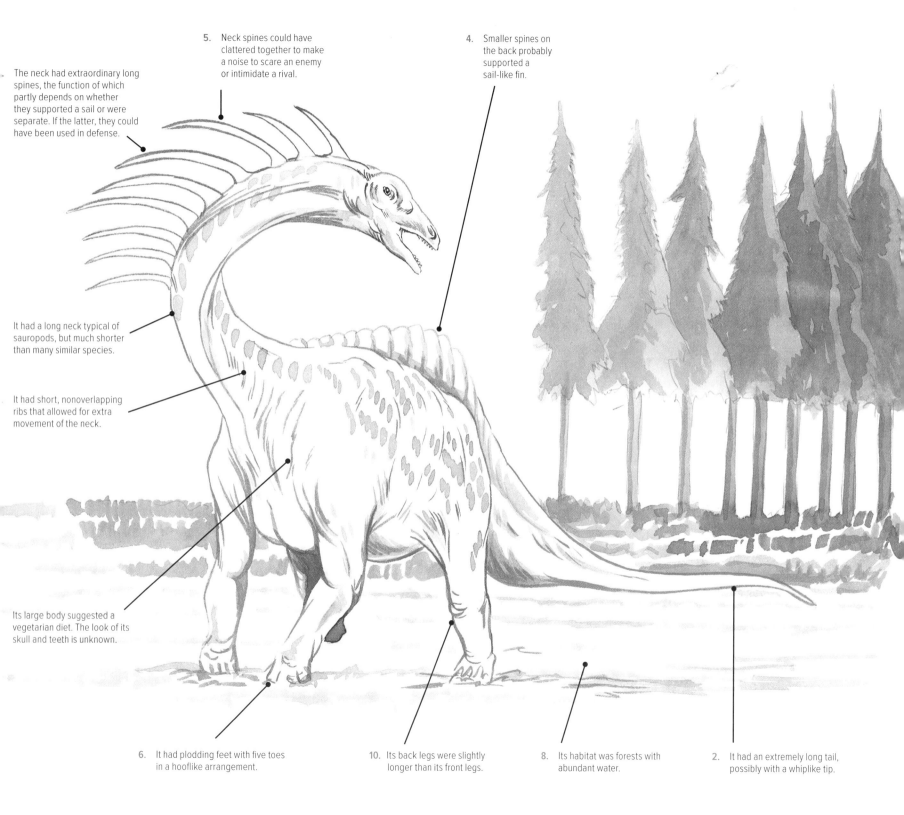

5. Neck spines could have clattered together to make a noise to scare an enemy or intimidate a rival.

4. Smaller spines on the back probably supported a sail-like fin.

The neck had extraordinary long spines, the function of which partly depends on whether they supported a sail or were separate. If the latter, they could have been used in defense.

It had a long neck typical of sauropods, but much shorter than many similar species.

It had short, nonoverlapping ribs that allowed for extra movement of the neck.

Its large body suggested a vegetarian diet. The look of its skull and teeth is unknown.

6. It had plodding feet with five toes in a hooflike arrangement.

10. Its back legs were slightly longer than its front legs.

8. Its habitat was forests with abundant water.

2. It had an extremely long tail, possibly with a whiplike tip.

Archaeoceratops | *Archaeoceratops oshiami*

Early Cretaceous, China • 125–112 million years ago • 3 feet (0.9 m) long

ARCHAEOCERATOPS IS SO SMALL that it looks more like a baby Triceratops than an ancestor of one. However, a forerunner is what it was, a member of an obscure group called the protoceratopsians that predated the famous large and heavy-horned dinosaurs from the late Cretaceous period. This particular creature was possibly the smallest of its kind, less than 3 feet (1 m) long, and it could presumably hide away in heavy brush, concealed from large predators.

Later Ceratopsians developed impressive horns and neck frills, but Archaeoceratops was modestly endowed. It had a small frill at the back of the skull for the protection of its head, but no horns. Even so, its head was still large for the animal's size, and it had an impressive beak that could break off all kinds of vegetation. There were a few teeth at the front of the jaw, as well as a battery at the back for grinding plant material.

It is not certain how this animal moved, because the two known skeletons lack arms. If it had short arms, it could have been able to run on two feet, a skill lost in its more lumbering relatives. If its arms were longer, it would have been quadripedal. Until more fossils are found, though, we won't know for sure.

10 THINGS TO REMEMBER

1. Its head was large for the size of its body.
2. Archaeoceratops had a few teeth at the front of its jaw, which were lost in later species.
3. Its eyes were shaded by an overhanging rim of bone.
4. It had no horn (most of its relatives had these).
5. It ate a vegetarian diet, probably ferns, cycads, and conifers.
6. It was almost certainly able to browse by rearing up on its hind feet.
7. Its toes were tipped with hooves. It might have been able to trot.
8. It had a sharp beak for snipping off vegetation, including coarse leaves and fruit.
9. It was probably able to run on two feet.
10. The bony frill protected the back of the head.

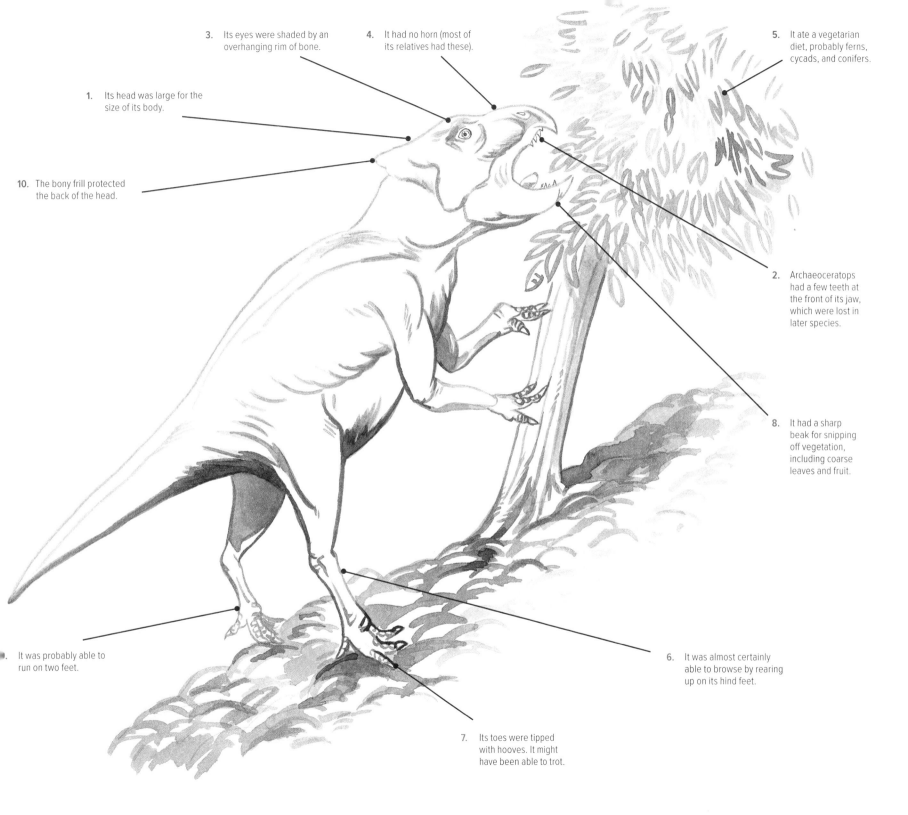

3. Its eyes were shaded by an overhanging rim of bone.

4. It had no horn (most of its relatives had these).

5. It ate a vegetarian diet, probably ferns, cycads, and conifers.

1. Its head was large for the size of its body.

10. The bony frill protected the back of the head.

2. Archaeoceratops had a few teeth at the front of its jaw, which were lost in later species.

8. It had a sharp beak for snipping off vegetation, including coarse leaves and fruit.

9. It was probably able to run on two feet.

6. It was almost certainly able to browse by rearing up on its hind feet.

7. Its toes were tipped with hooves. It might have been able to trot.

Argentinosaurus | *Argentinosaurus huinculensis*

Early Cretaceous, Argentina • 97–94 million years ago • 100–115 feet (30–35 m) long

ARGENTINOSAURUS IS INVOLVED IN ONE OF THE GREAT DEBATES of modern paleonotology. Exactly which one was the biggest dinosaur that ever existed? Quite a few enormous, lumbering sauropods compete for the title, but it is generally accepted that Argentinosaurus is the frontrunner. As such, it can be considered as having been the largest land animal of all. One intriguing aspect of the debate is that Argentinosaurus is known from an extremely paltry set of bones—a selection of vertebrae and ribs, plus a tibia and femur (two leg bones). It is only by comparing the size of these bones to better-known sauropod skeletons that the dimensions of Argentinosaurus were figured out in a case of informed guesswork. This result came to an estimate of between 100–115 feet (30–35 m).

Unsurprisingly, in addition to size, this animal was also heavy. It probably reached about 77 tons (70 metric tonnes) when fully grown. Bearing in mind that it hatched from a small egg—probably weighing only 11 pounds (5 kg) at birth, it is quite an increase in weight for an animal that may have lived only a few decades. Another mind-boggling piece of guesswork concluded that, at the height of its growth phase, it could have gained 100 pounds (45 kg) every single day!

Interestingly, Argentinosaurus lived much later than what is considered to be the golden age of gigantic sauropods, the late Jurassic. However, at the time of Argentinosaurus's existence, South America was isolated as an island continent, meaning a slightly different set of evolutionary rules.

10 THINGS TO REMEMBER

1. It is thought to be the largest dinosaur, measuring up to 115 feet (35 m) long.

2. Enormously long neck was adapted for browsing from all heights of trees, including the tallest.

3. Its extreme bulk may also have been able to push over trees, to make it easy to get at the leaves.

4. It had four columnar, elephant-like legs, needed to support its massive weight.

5. Its relatively tiny head would have been necessary to cut down weight at the top of the neck.

6. Blood vessels inside the neck would need to have been broad to allow blood flow to the brain against gravity. It would also have needed valves to ensure that the blood did not flow down again.

7. Its teeth remain unknown, but it would have probably not been particularly choosy in its diet—it had to eat all day, every day.

8. Its feet would have had hooves, to bear the animal's weight.

9. Its sheer bulk probably prevented any predator from attacking an adult, but juveniles would have been a possible target.

10. It may have needed to avoid ground that was too soft, to prevent it from sinking due to its weight.

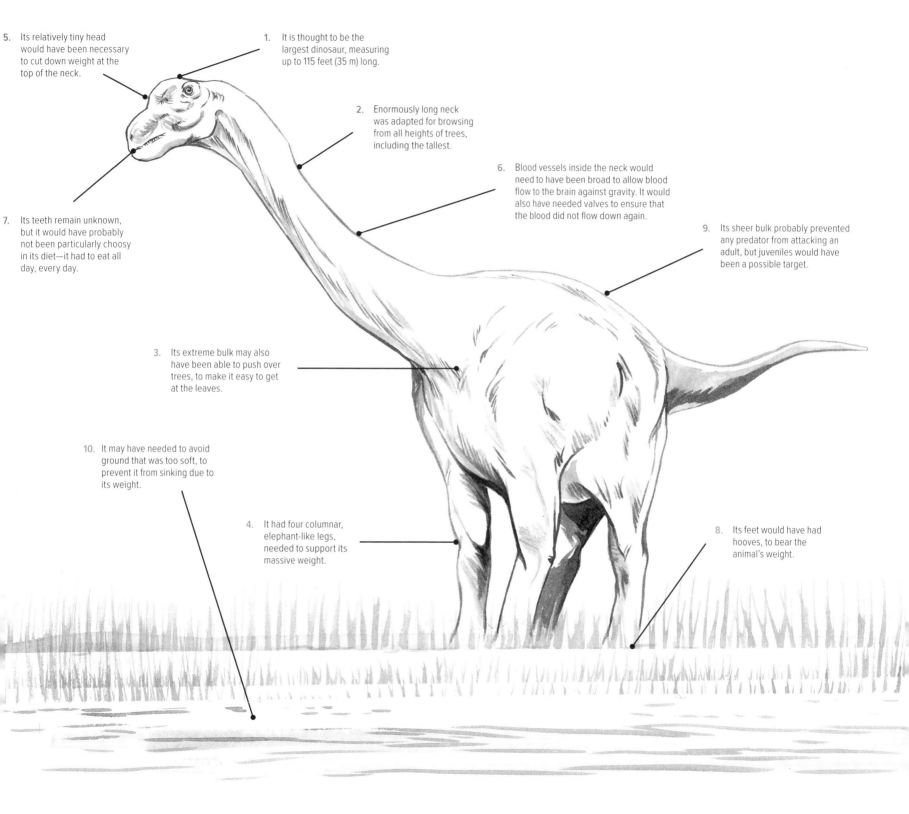

5. Its relatively tiny head would have been necessary to cut down weight at the top of the neck.

1. It is thought to be the largest dinosaur, measuring up to 115 feet (35 m) long.

2. Enormously long neck was adapted for browsing from all heights of trees, including the tallest.

6. Blood vessels inside the neck would need to have been broad to allow blood flow to the brain against gravity. It would also have needed valves to ensure that the blood did not flow down again.

7. Its teeth remain unknown, but it would have probably not been particularly choosy in its diet—it had to eat all day, every day.

9. Its sheer bulk probably prevented any predator from attacking an adult, but juveniles would have been a possible target.

3. Its extreme bulk may also have been able to push over trees, to make it easy to get at the leaves.

10. It may have needed to avoid ground that was too soft, to prevent it from sinking due to its weight.

4. It had four columnar, elephant-like legs, needed to support its massive weight.

8. Its feet would have had hooves, to bear the animal's weight.

Quetzalcoatlus | *Quetzalcoatlus northropi*

Late Cretaceous, U.S.A. (Texas) • 68–65 million years ago • Wingspan 33–36 feet (10–11 m)

IT IS BROADLY AGREED THAT QUETZALCOATLUS had the widest wingspan of any known animal, at least 33 feet (10 m) from tip to tip. What is not as clear is whether this pterosaur actually did any significant flying. Recent studies indicate that it spent a lot of time on the ground, walking on all fours. But if so, why did it have such enormous wings? The truth is that, for the moment, the gigantic Quetzalcoatlus remains a mysterious creature.

However, what does seem to have been ruled out is powered flight. The weight of the animal is not known for sure, but it is thought to have been too great for this type of flight. However, on the Cretaceous plains of Texas, there would have been strong air currents and thermals to help Quetzalcoatlus soar. Some biologists think that it might have had a lifestyle similar to today's vulture, remaining high aloft to look for dead flesh; however, the bill probably was not strong or sharp enough to cope with tough animal hides. Another possibility is that it stalked along the ground looking for small animals.

Nothing is known about the reproduction of this outsize pterosaur, but it does seem highly likely that both the bill and the crest on top of its head were colorful, the latter perhaps enlarged during the breeding season to attract a mate.

10 THINGS TO REMEMBER

1. It had a very long, sharp beak, similar to that of a modern-day stork.

2. It lacked teeth, in contrast to earlier pterosaurs.

3. Its crest was probably ornate and colorful, although the details are not known.

4. It was a predator of small animals of all kinds. This one is raiding a nest of sauropod dinosaurs.

5. It had a thick neck that was 10 feet (3 m) long.

6. It had a short tail.

7. Its enormous wings dwarfed its small body.

8. The vastly elongated fourth finger made up the tip of the wing, with a thick membrane of skin making the rest.

9. Despite their awkward appearance, the length of the limbs suggests that it could have walked efficiently and quickly.

10. It had sharp claws on its forelimbs.

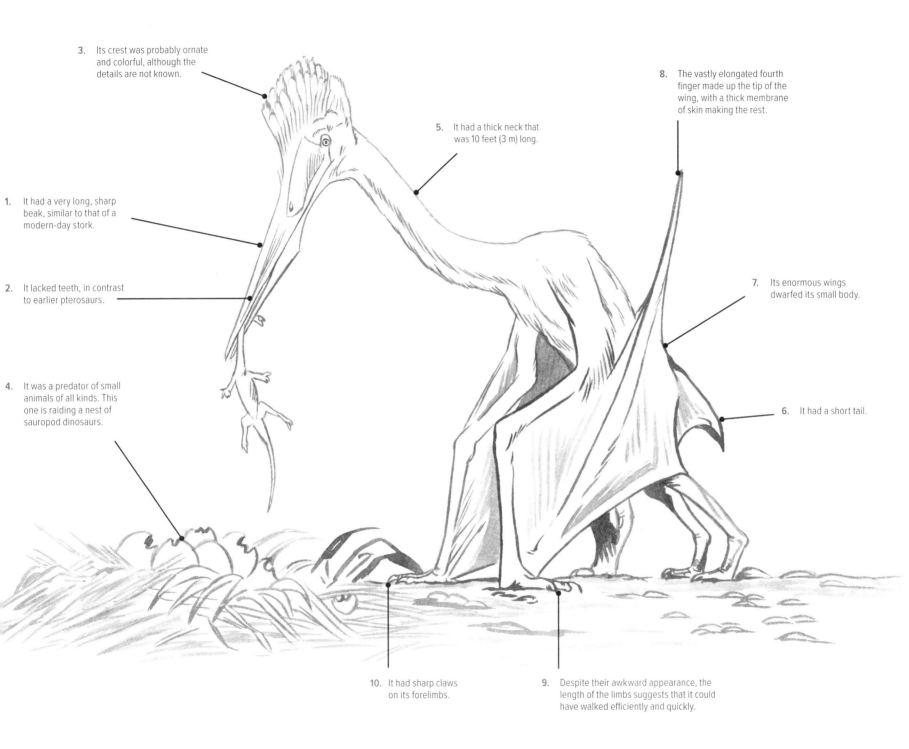

3. Its crest was probably ornate and colorful, although the details are not known.

8. The vastly elongated fourth finger made up the tip of the wing, with a thick membrane of skin making the rest.

5. It had a thick neck that was 10 feet (3 m) long.

1. It had a very long, sharp beak, similar to that of a modern-day stork.

2. It lacked teeth, in contrast to earlier pterosaurs.

7. Its enormous wings dwarfed its small body.

4. It was a predator of small animals of all kinds. This one is raiding a nest of sauropod dinosaurs.

6. It had a short tail.

10. It had sharp claws on its forelimbs.

9. Despite their awkward appearance, the length of the limbs suggests that it could have walked efficiently and quickly.

Spinosaurus | *Spinosaurus aegypticus*

Late Cretaceous, Egypt • 100–95 million years ago • 46 feet (14 m) long

IT IS ENTIRELY POSSIBLE THAT SPINOSAURUS was the largest land predator ever to have walked the Earth. It was at least 46 feet (14 m) long, and its skull alone measured 6.5 feet (2 m)—the height of a human being; rivals such as Carcharodontosaurus and Tyrannosaurus were shorter but probably heavier.

This awesome predator was unique in many ways. Not only did it have an unusual long snout armed with teeth adapted more for grabbing than slicing, it also boasted a large sail along its back, held up with vertical spines of up to 6.5 feet (2 m) long. The function of this sail is unknown, as is the case for other dinosaurs with similar structures, such as Ouranosaurus. It might have been colorful and used for signaling, or it could have been used in heat regulation, or both.

The story of the Spinosaurus fossils is almost as interesting as the animal itself. The first remains, including parts of the skull and spines, were found in Egypt in 1912 by the German fossil hunter Ernst Stromer. They immediately caused a sensation, since nothing of their kind had been found before. Unfortunately, however, all traces of Spinosaurus were destroyed in an Allied bombing raid on Munich, Germany, in 1944, leaving only Stromer's notes and illustrations to record its existence. The dinosaur almost became extinct twice, but since 1971 some other fragmentary material has been discovered, most particularly a skull in Morocco in 1996.

10 THINGS TO REMEMBER

1. It had a very long, shallow head with an elongated snout.
2. The tip of the lower jaw expanded to increase its reach and the span of its jaws.
3. The teeth were conical and not serrated. It is thought that they were used mainly for grabbing prey.
4. Recent detailed chemical studies of the teeth suggest that Spinosaurus was semiaquatic.
5. The crocodile-like jaws suggested that fish were probably a major prey animal.
6. Sharp claws on its arms may have been the major predatory weapons.
7. Large spines sticking up from the backbone made a sail.
8. The sail may have been colorful and used to signal others of the species.
9. It walked bipedally, like other large predatory theropods.
10. The relatively flexible upper spine possibly allowed the sail to be arched or even spread.

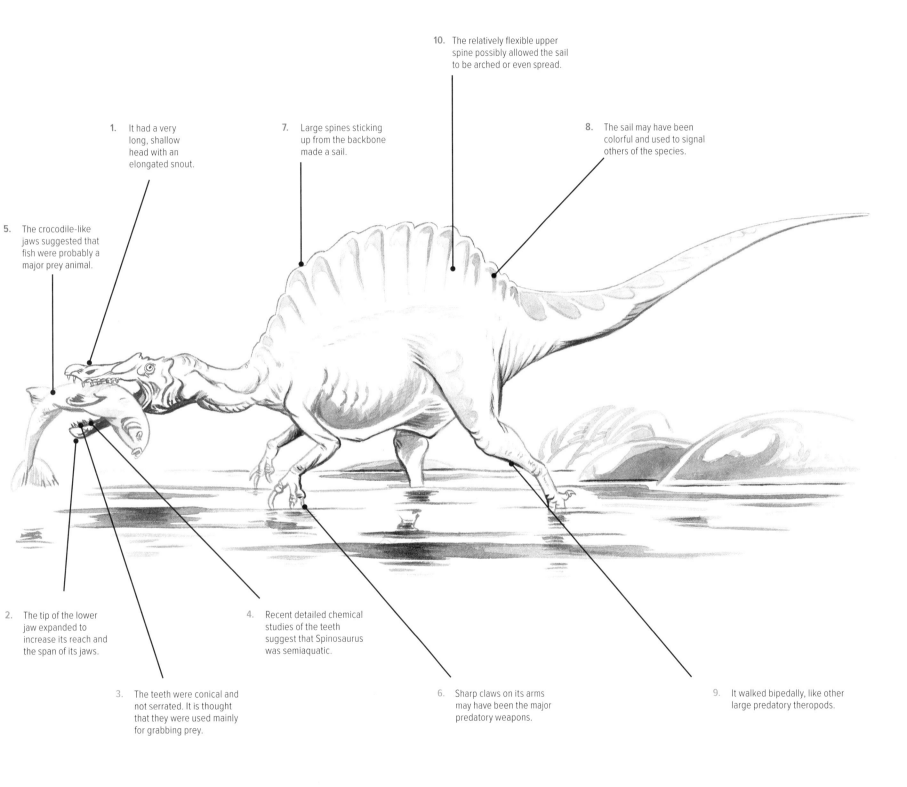

10. The relatively flexible upper spine possibly allowed the sail to be arched or even spread.

1. It had a very long, shallow head with an elongated snout.

7. Large spines sticking up from the backbone made a sail.

8. The sail may have been colorful and used to signal others of the species.

5. The crocodile-like jaws suggested that fish were probably a major prey animal.

2. The tip of the lower jaw expanded to increase its reach and the span of its jaws.

4. Recent detailed chemical studies of the teeth suggest that Spinosaurus was semiaquatic.

3. The teeth were conical and not serrated. It is thought that they were used mainly for grabbing prey.

6. Sharp claws on its arms may have been the major predatory weapons.

9. It walked bipedally, like other large predatory theropods.

Carcharodontosaurus | *Carcharodontosaurus saharicus*

Late Cretaceous, Egypt and Morocco • 100–95 million years ago • 40 feet (12 m) long

THIS ANIMAL'S LONG NAME SIMPLY MEANS "shark-toothed lizard." If this dinosaur ambushed you, you would be devoured before you could say its name. Its teeth were up to 8 inches (20 cm) long, thin, bladelike, and serrated, and could inflict fatal wounds, even on the toughest flesh. There were 14 teeth on either side of the upper jaw, and they had grooves at the side to allow blood to flow away. This dinosaur was a hunter, and one of the most formidable ever known. It is thought to have been slightly bigger than a Tyrannosaurus, with an appetite to match. But Carcharodontosaurus had a much smaller brain than Tyrannosaurus, so at least it was not as intelligent.

Scientists have estimated that this animal might have run as fast as 20 miles per hour (32 km/h) based on fossilized trackways, but it is highly unlikely that it ever managed to get to such a speed. Carcharodontosaurus, as you can see in the picture, had remarkably small, apparently useless arms. If it tripped and fell, its arms could not protect it, and a major slip could have resulted in permanent damage.

You might think that one A-list carnivore was enough for a single ecosystem, but astonishingly, this outsize theropod shared its North African seaside mangrove swamps with the equally gigantic Spinosaurus. The two would have undoubtedly met up and perhaps fought occasionally, but Spinosaurus primarily ate fish and Carcharodontosaurus mainly attacked dinosaurs on land.

10 THINGS TO REMEMBER

1. Extremely small arms could not have broken its fall if this dinosaur tripped. Some predatory dinosaurs show broken and then healed ribs, probably caused by a fall.

2. The arms had sharp claws that could have done damage.

3. The largest teeth were up to 8 inches (20 cm) long (smaller than Tyrannosaurus, but formidable).

4. The teeth were thin, bladelike, and serrated, like a shark's.

5. It had a long, heavy skull adapted for dealing with large prey animals.

6. It has been found in coastal areas with mangrove swamps, so it might have hunted by the waterside.

7. It had a smaller brain cavity than Tyrannosaurus, indicating that it was not such a clever hunter.

8. It ran on two very large muscular legs, as was common for a large, meat-eating theropod.

9. It had three load-bearing toes on its feet, one small and raised.

10. It had bony ridges on top of its head.

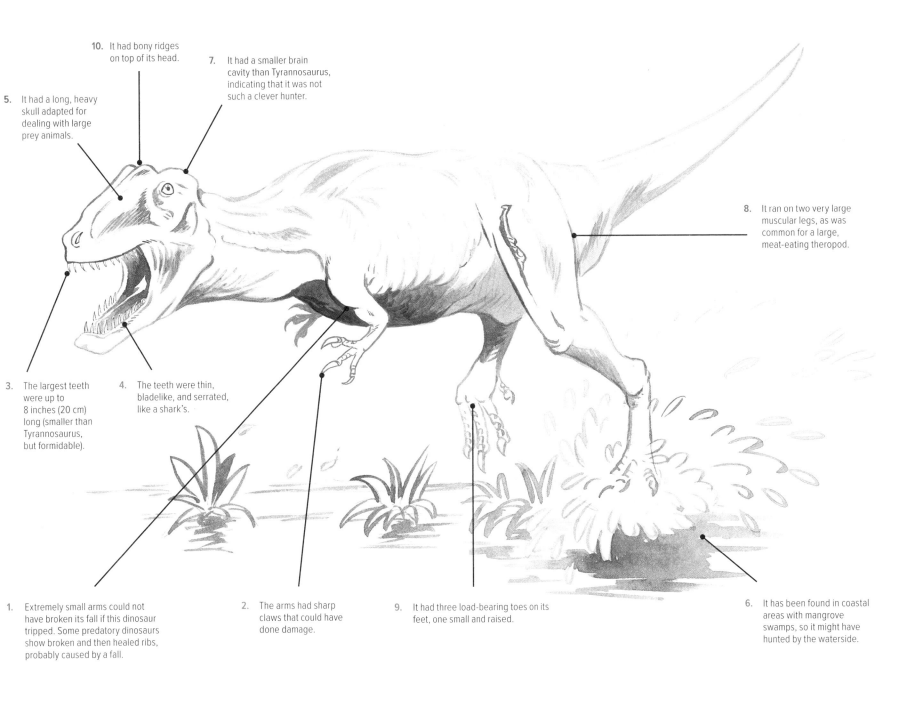

10. It had bony ridges on top of its head.

7. It had a smaller brain cavity than Tyrannosaurus, indicating that it was not such a clever hunter.

5. It had a long, heavy skull adapted for dealing with large prey animals.

8. It ran on two very large muscular legs, as was common for a large, meat-eating theropod.

3. The largest teeth were up to 8 inches (20 cm) long (smaller than Tyrannosaurus, but formidable).

4. The teeth were thin, bladelike, and serrated, like a shark's.

1. Extremely small arms could not have broken its fall if this dinosaur tripped. Some predatory dinosaurs show broken and then healed ribs, probably caused by a fall.

2. The arms had sharp claws that could have done damage.

9. It had three load-bearing toes on its feet, one small and raised.

6. It has been found in coastal areas with mangrove swamps, so it might have hunted by the waterside.

Tyrannosaurus | *Tyrannosaurus rex*

Late Cretaceous, U.S.A. (Midwest) • 67–65 million years ago • 40 feet (12 m) long

SO ICONIC IS THE WORLD'S MOST FAMOUS DINOSAUR, and such a familiar part of our culture in books, movies, and TV shows, that it is sometimes easy to forget that it is extinct! Tyrannosaurus rex did not rule the world—only the Midwest—but its fame derives from its ability to have caught the imagination of fossil hunters and public alike in the mid-twentieth century.

T. rex was certainly a huge, carnivorous, deadly predator, and almost the largest of its kind. Its skull was simply enormous, at almost 5 feet (1.5 m) in length, and massively built and powered by large muscles. There were more than 50 teeth of exceptional size, some as long as 1 foot (30 cm). Its front teeth were D-shaped and built for gripping, while the back teeth were thin and sharp. Wear marks on teeth from Tyrannosaurus prove that, unusually among dinosaurs, this animal could actually bite through bone. Also unusually, it did not slash at its prey; instead it made deep, direct bites aimed at a quick kill.

How it was able to catch up with its food is still not firmly established, although it is thought that it used ambush techniques. However, some scientists have suggested it was mainly a scavenger, eating dead meat. Adults certainly ate the largest available food, and some of this was slow-moving, including Triceratops, and, in the south of its range, large sauropods.

The 30 or so known Tyrannosaurus skeletons show a variety of forms and growth stages. These include two different adult shapes—a "gracile" morph and a "robust" morph. It is possible that the larger, heavier-headed robust morph is the female. Juveniles had longer legs and arms and were probably fast runners, formidable in their own right.

10 THINGS TO REMEMBER

1. The eyes faced partially forward, giving binocular vision (overlapping fields of view that allowed for perception of distance).

2. Nostrils set in a broad snout led to very large olfactory lobes in the brain, resulting in an excellent sense of smell.

3. The skull was box-shaped to accommodate exceptionally powerful jaw muscles.

4. Arms were small, and their function was obscure. They might have been used by males to grip when mating.

5. Marks left on skull fossils suggest that individuals may have used these to headbutt each other during disputes.

6. The scales on the skin were small and had the appearance of stones in a mosaic.

7. Enormous teeth were up to 1 foot (30 cm) long. They were used to bite through flesh and bone.

8. It had a relative short, light tail compared to other similar theropods. The tail was raised above the ground and acted as counterbalance, allowing the animal to turn.

9. Legs were relatively long and strong. Maximum running speeds have been estimated at around 25 miles per hour (40 km/h).

10. The neck was very broad and robust.

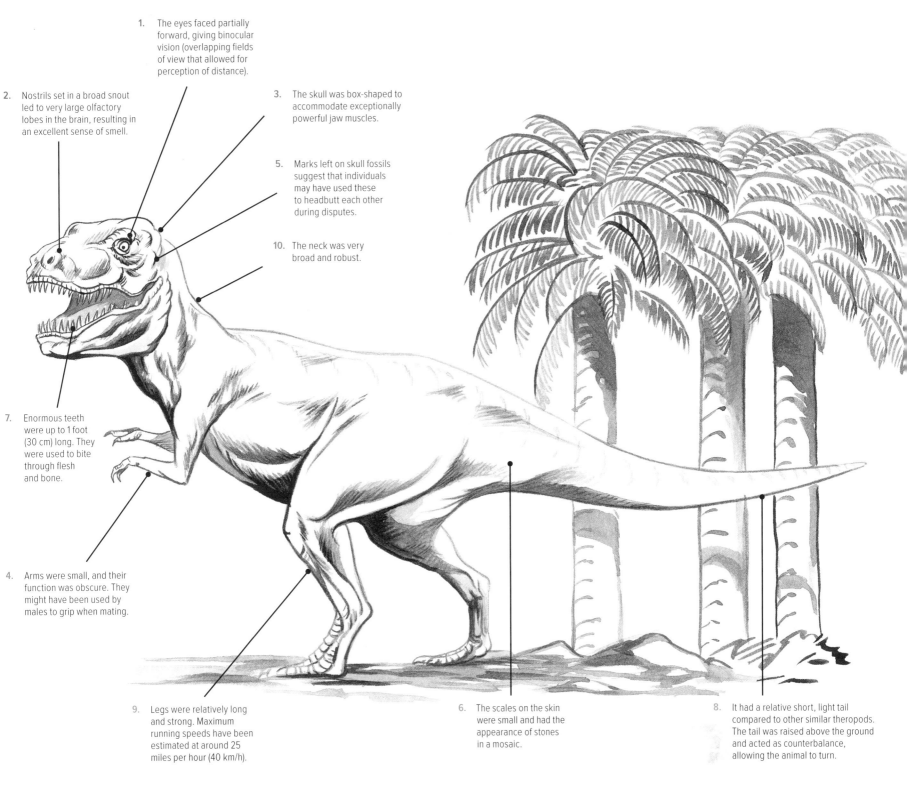

1. The eyes faced partially forward, giving binocular vision (overlapping fields of view that allowed for perception of distance).

2. Nostrils set in a broad snout led to very large olfactory lobes in the brain, resulting in an excellent sense of smell.

3. The skull was box-shaped to accommodate exceptionally powerful jaw muscles.

5. Marks left on skull fossils suggest that individuals may have used these to headbutt each other during disputes.

10. The neck was very broad and robust.

7. Enormous teeth were up to 1 foot (30 cm) long. They were used to bite through flesh and bone.

4. Arms were small, and their function was obscure. They might have been used by males to grip when mating.

9. Legs were relatively long and strong. Maximum running speeds have been estimated at around 25 miles per hour (40 km/h).

6. The scales on the skin were small and had the appearance of stones in a mosaic.

8. It had a relative short, light tail compared to other similar theropods. The tail was raised above the ground and acted as counterbalance, allowing the animal to turn.

Triceratops | *Triceratops horridus*

Late Cretaceous, U.S.A. (Midwest) • 68–65 million years ago • 26 feet (8 m) long

THE SEISMIC BATTLES BETWEEN THE GREAT HORNED DINOSAUR Triceratops and its nemesis Tyrannosaurus have long caught the imagination of dinosaur enthusiasts and the general public alike. These skirmishes did undoubtedly happen, as these two superstars were found in the same time and place, and horns of Triceratops have been found that were bitten before healing. Poignantly, however, at this thrilling apogee of dinosaur evolution, the age of dinosaurs quite suddenly came to an end. Individual Triceratops and Tyrannosaurus probably witnessed the asteroid strike that wiped out their dynasty and began a new chapter of Earth's history.

Triceratops was the largest member of the group of horned dinosaurs known as ceratopsids. It was distinctive for having three horns: two long ones just above the eyes (brow horns) and a rhinoceros-like nasal horn. It also had a frill at the back of the skull, which is thought to have grown larger with age. More subtly, it also had different skin to its relatives, with bigger scales that were often raised, giving it an irregular, pitted appearance.

At the center of current controversy are the two close relatives Triceratops and Torosaurus (see page 88). It has been suggested that the two may actually be the same creature, but this theory remains hotly debated.

There is little doubt that the head armor played its role in the defense of a Triceratops, but there is every chance that these adornments also played a prominent role in sexual selection and display. Rivals doubtless locked horns in combat, and the frills were probably colorful and may have been variable between the sexes.

10 THINGS TO REMEMBER

1. Triceratops lived alongside Tyrannosaurus, and life-and-death battles between the two certainly took place.

2. Two large brow horns (up to 3 feet/1 m long) could inflict wounds on an enemy.

3. It had a large nasal horn.

4. It had a large frill at the back of its skull. This is thought to have grown larger with age and was probably an important part of individual display to other members of the species.

5. It had three hooves on its front legs.

6. It had large body scales, many with raised cones.

7. Its head was low to the ground, so it was probably confined to browsing the lowest vegetation. However, it might have been able to knock down vegetation.

8. It had a deep, narrow beak, possibly adapted for grasping.

9. It had a shorter tail than many of its relatives.

10. Its short legs suggest that it was a slow-moving dinosaur.

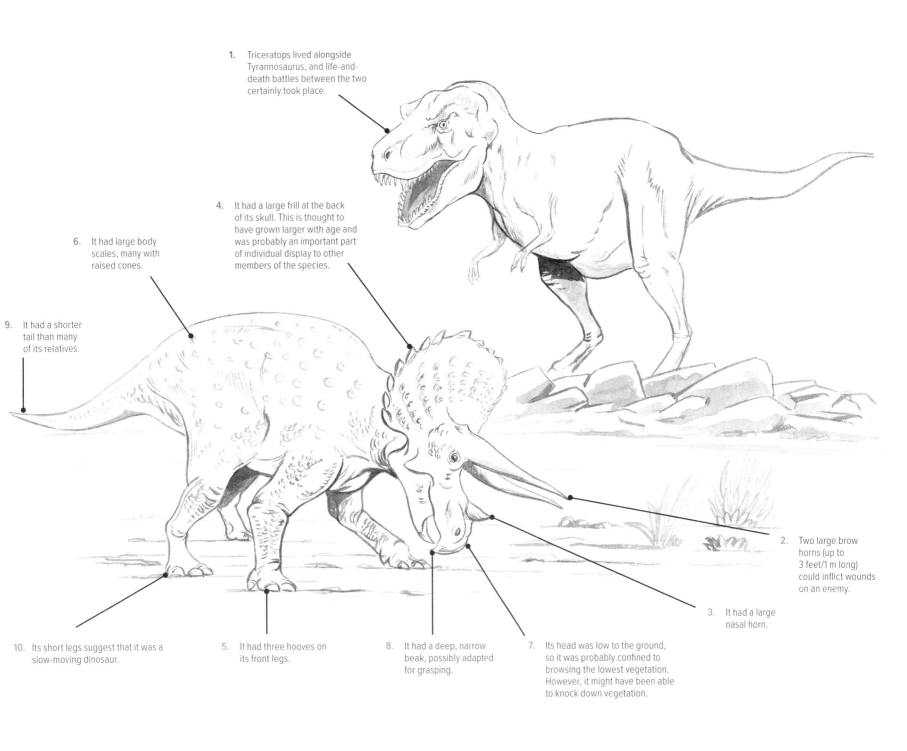

1. Triceratops lived alongside Tyrannosaurus, and life-and-death battles between the two certainly took place.

4. It had a large frill at the back of its skull. This is thought to have grown larger with age and was probably an important part of individual display to other members of the species.

6. It had large body scales, many with raised cones.

9. It had a shorter tail than many of its relatives.

2. Two large brow horns (up to 3 feet/1 m long) could inflict wounds on an enemy.

3. It had a large nasal horn.

10. Its short legs suggest that it was a slow-moving dinosaur.

5. It had three hooves on its front legs.

8. It had a deep, narrow beak, possibly adapted for grasping.

7. Its head was low to the ground, so it was probably confined to browsing the lowest vegetation. However, it might have been able to knock down vegetation.

Velociraptor | *Velociraptor mongoliensis*

Late Cretaceous, Mongolia and Northern China • 75–71 million years ago • 8 feet (2.5 m) long

ALTHOUGH A FAR CRY FROM THE MUCH LARGER ANIMALS depicted as Velociraptors in *Jurassic Park* (those were actually Deinonychus, page 56), Velociraptor still fits the description of a dangerous and highly advanced predator, a kind of roadrunner from hell. Light in body and quick on its feet, it could probably have run at 40 miles per hour (64 km/h) in short bursts, and its extremely long tail ensured that it was able to turn rapidly. A Velociraptor, or even a pack of them, chasing after you probably meant that your end was near.

It was a common predator in its desert environment in Mongolia and China, and that is likely to have meant that it could eat almost anything, large and small. One of the world's most famous fossils, of a Velociraptor locked in combat with a Protoceratops, proves that it would tackle an animal of similar size and weighing as much as 380 pounds (172 kg), but it is safe to assume that most prey animals were much smaller. Velociraptor would have been adaptable, and its large brain would have ensured that it could figure out strategies for capture, including ambush. One recently discovered fossil showed a Velociraptor with the bone of a large pterosaur in its intestines, although it seems likely that this was obtained by scavenging the carcass, rather than by killing it.

There is some evidence that raptors such as Velociraptor worked together, but that does not mean they always got along. One Velociraptor specimen showed punctures in its skull that fit the teeth of its own species—showing that it was probably killed in a fight with its own kind.

10 THINGS TO REMEMBER

1. It could be distinguished from other raptors by its long snout.

2. The snout was slightly upturned, to increase the reach of its jaws.

3. The large, sickle-shaped claws on its back legs were its main weapon for killing prey. They might also have been useful for climbing onto the backs of larger animals.

4. Quill nodes on the upper arm of fossils prove that it had feathers, presumably arranged into a wing.

5. It was probably a generalist predator, able to catch prey of various sizes. This small pterosaur would have made a large meal.

6. It possessed 80 very sharp, curved teeth.

7. The extremely long tail enabled it to balance while running, especially when turning.

8. It lived in a desert, with dunes.

9. It probably had feathers covering most of its body as insulation, although there is no direct evidence for this.

10. Its very light body and small size suggested that it was a fast runner.

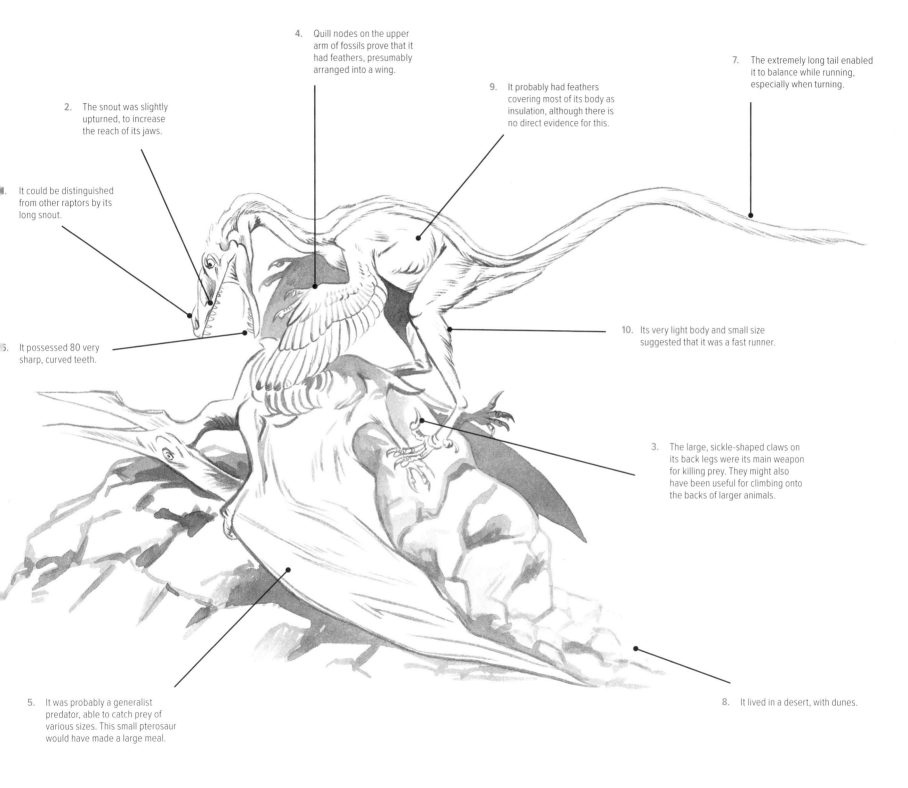

4. Quill nodes on the upper arm of fossils prove that it had feathers, presumably arranged into a wing.

9. It probably had feathers covering most of its body as insulation, although there is no direct evidence for this.

7. The extremely long tail enabled it to balance while running, especially when turning.

2. The snout was slightly upturned, to increase the reach of its jaws.

1. It could be distinguished from other raptors by its long snout.

6. It possessed 80 very sharp, curved teeth.

10. Its very light body and small size suggested that it was a fast runner.

3. The large, sickle-shaped claws on its back legs were its main weapon for killing prey. They might also have been useful for climbing onto the backs of larger animals.

5. It was probably a generalist predator, able to catch prey of various sizes. This small pterosaur would have made a large meal.

8. It lived in a desert, with dunes.

Protoceratops | *Protoceratops andrewsi*

Late Cretaceous, Mongolia • 86–71 million years ago • 8 feet (2.5 m) long

PROTOCERATOPS IS BEST KNOWN FOR BEING FOSSILIZED IN THE HEIGHT OF BATTLE. One of the world's most famous finds, unearthed in Mongolia in 1971, preserved the remains of a Protoceratops and a Velociraptor locked in mortal combat, the Protoceratops biting the arm of the aggressor, and the Velociraptor's claw embedded in its victim's throat. The two animals were presumably rapidly engulfed by a collapsing sand dune, and they provide a unique snapshot of prehistoric predation.

This animal is unmistakably similar in basic form to its better-known relatives, such as Triceratops, but it is much smaller and less ornamented. It did have a large frill on the back of its neck, and a small horn above its nose, plus its head was typically armored and large, accounting for one-fifth of the length of the animal. Its eyes were surprisingly large, indicating that it had excellent eyesight and might even have been active in twilight. Like its relatives, it was an herbivore.

Recently, a fossilized brood of Protoceratops hatchlings was discovered in Mongolia. There are 15 altogether, evidently gathered into a nest, suggesting that this dinosaur might have cared for its young, at least in the early stages.

A curious footnote to this animal's existence is that it is possible that it gave rise to the legend of the griffin. These mythical creatures, four-footed and with birdlike beaks, may have been inspired by well-preserved dinosaur skulls found by traders in Central Asia.

10 THINGS TO REMEMBER

1. Beaklike jaws would have been able to deliver a powerful bite.

2. Its enormous head accounts for one-fifth of the length of the entire animal.

3. It had a small nasal horn, perhaps used in territorial combat. Later relatives had much larger horns.

4. It had a wide frill at the back of its skull, with two holes to reduce the weight. This could have also protected the neck.

5. It possessed teeth near the front of its jaw (a primitive feature) and a battery of teeth toward the back.

6. It lived in a desert habitat.

7. It walked around on all four limbs.

8. It had tall vertebral spines over its tail. Their function is unknown.

9. It had large eyes and may have seen well in low light levels.

10. It had longer limbs than some relatives, so it might have moved faster or traveled farther.

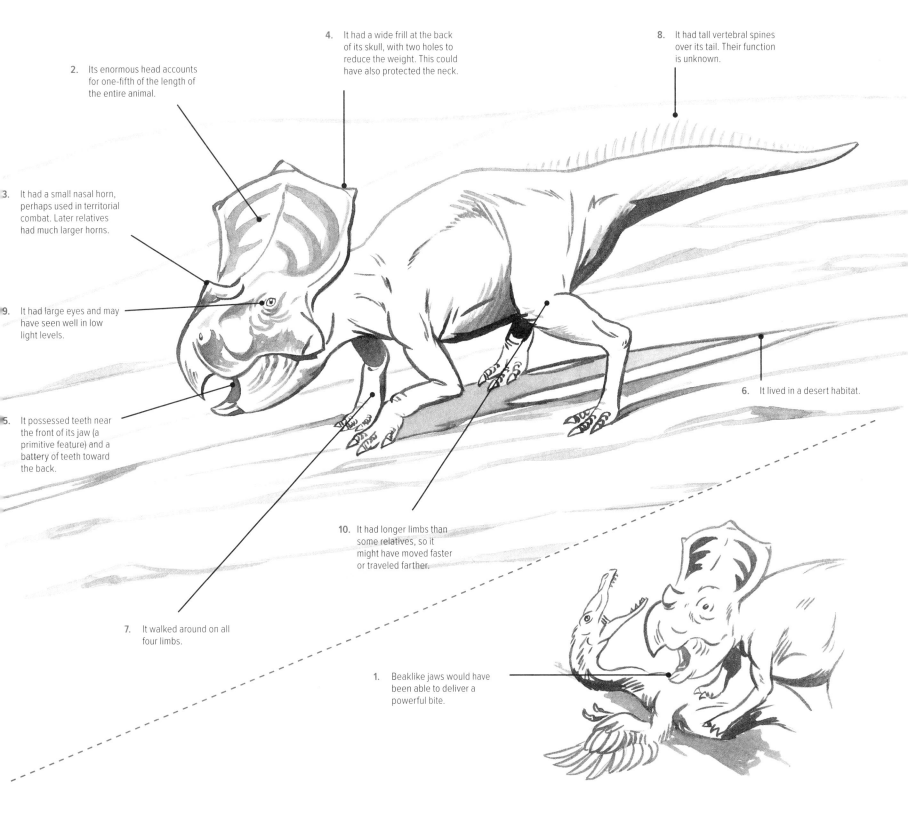

2. Its enormous head accounts for one-fifth of the length of the entire animal.

4. It had a wide frill at the back of its skull, with two holes to reduce the weight. This could have also protected the neck.

8. It had tall vertebral spines over its tail. Their function is unknown.

3. It had a small nasal horn, perhaps used in territorial combat. Later relatives had much larger horns.

9. It had large eyes and may have seen well in low light levels.

5. It possessed teeth near the front of its jaw (a primitive feature) and a battery of teeth toward the back.

6. It lived in a desert habitat.

10. It had longer limbs than some relatives, so it might have moved faster or traveled farther.

7. It walked around on all four limbs.

1. Beaklike jaws would have been able to deliver a powerful bite.

Pachycephalosaurus | *Pachycephalosaurus wyomingensis*

Late Cretaceous, U.S.A. (Montana, South Dakota, Wyoming) • 75–71 million years ago • 15 feet (4.5 m) long

THIS IS A VERY STRANGE DINOSAUR with a number of mysterious features. The most obvious is the extraordinary dome-headed skull, surrounded by a ridge of knobs at its base, some of which are elongated into spikes. However, aspects of the teeth and tail are also unusual, combining to make this a very odd creature.

You cannot miss the outsize dome on the head of Pachycephalosaurus (this is what gave it the scientific name meaning "thick-headed lizard"), and scientists have spent years speculating about what it was for. The obvious function would be to headbutt an opponent or rival, but there is considerable doubt as to whether this happened—no fossilized skulls have any evidence of broken or healed segments, as you would normally expect from this kind of engagement. It is more likely that the skulls were used as ornaments to attract the opposite sex and to intimidate opponents; viewed head-on, they are impressive. It is likely that they were brightly colored.

The teeth of Pachycephalosaurus are also interesting, because they are not conventional herbivorous teeth. They are small and leaf-shaped, inside a short beak. They probably indicate an omnivorous diet, with some animal as well as plant material. The tail, meanwhile, was unusual for its complex, woven-basket-type latticework of bone-hard tendons along the last two-thirds of its length, presumably to strengthen it.

10 THINGS TO REMEMBER

1. Outsize dome was on top of the skull. This could have been a display organ or for hitting an enemy or rival on the side.

2. Knobs adorned the base of the skull. In some individuals these became spikes, possibly used in combat between individuals.

3. It had spikes at the base of its nostrils.

4. Its beak was very short, with limited reach. It may have low-browsed or eaten nonplant material.

5. The teeth were small and leaflike. These would have been good for stripping leaves off branches, as well as for processing some animal food.

6. There were five fingers on each arm, so the animal may have been able to hold branches and break them off.

7. It had four long toes equipped with blunt claws.

8. It had a fairly long, S-shaped neck (this would have broken easily in head-to-head combat).

9. The tail was raised from the ground and very strong, with an entire latticework of ossified tendons.

10. It had very broad hips to accommodate a large belly.

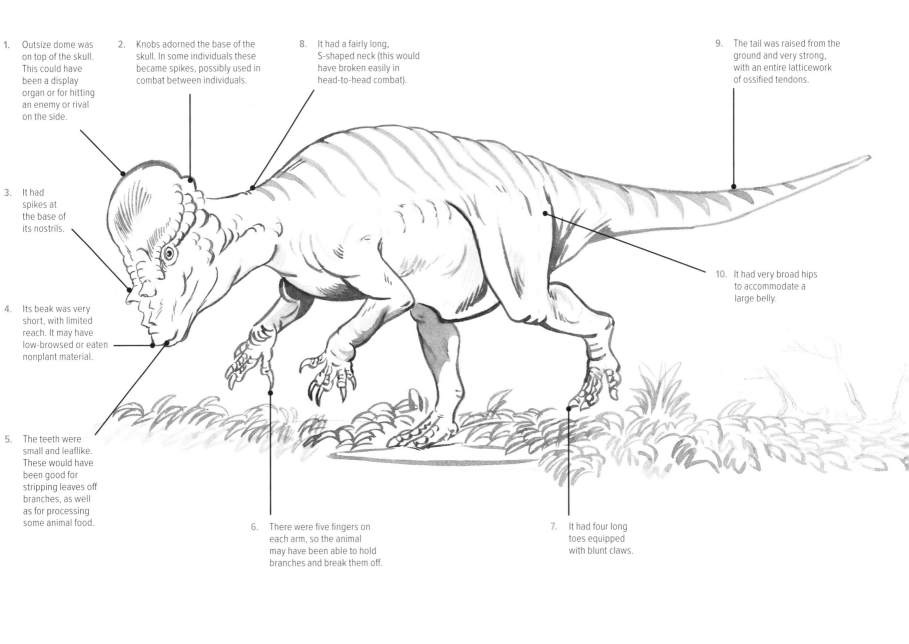

1. Outsize dome was on top of the skull. This could have been a display organ or for hitting an enemy or rival on the side.

2. Knobs adorned the base of the skull. In some individuals these became spikes, possibly used in combat between individuals.

8. It had a fairly long, S-shaped neck (this would have broken easily in head-to-head combat).

9. The tail was raised from the ground and very strong, with an entire latticework of ossified tendons.

3. It had spikes at the base of its nostrils.

4. Its beak was very short, with limited reach. It may have low-browsed or eaten nonplant material.

10. It had very broad hips to accommodate a large belly.

5. The teeth were small and leaflike. These would have been good for stripping leaves off branches, as well as for processing some animal food.

6. There were five fingers on each arm, so the animal may have been able to hold branches and break them off.

7. It had four long toes equipped with blunt claws.

Chasmosaurus | *Chasmosaurus russelli*

Late Cretaceous, Canada (Alberta) • 88–71 million years ago • 14 feet (4.3 m) long

ALTHOUGH THE BETTER-KNOWN TRICERATOPS HAD IMPRESSIVE HORNS, Chasmosaurus was big in the frill department. It did have three horns, a rhinoceros-like one on its nose and two short brow-horns, but the frill behind these was simply enormous and probably colorful—by far the most conspicuous part of the beast. It was roughly triangular, narrow toward the beak, and greatly widened toward the back and top, and the outside edges were decorated (or possibly armed?) with small spikes, the largest at the top corners. So large was this adornment that, presumably in order to save weight, the skeleton of the frill consisted simply of the outer edge and a single strut in the middle, with the rest presumably made up from soft tissue.

The animal illustrated here is just one species of Chasmosaurus, but there were at least three others with no brow horns or smaller frills. Interestingly, each of these species has been found at just one or two locations. This suggests the different species all had very small geographical ranges, a pattern that is often seen in living animals but is very rare in dinosaurs.

The slight differences in species also strongly suggest that all these frills and horns were primarily for show and perhaps just secondarily for protection. They probably varied between individuals and between the sexes, as well as between the species. It was a case of "by their frills you will know them."

10 THINGS TO REMEMBER

1. It had an enormous frill, probably for ornamentation to impress females or to intimidate rival males.

2. The center of the frill was hollow bone, to keep weight down.

3. The nasal horn may have been used in combat between species.

4. Two brow-horns (these are not present in Chasmosaurus irvinensis and are small in C. belli).

5. A very large, heavy, hooked beak allowed it to chew tough vegetation and may have played a part in defense.

6. It was small compared to Triceratops.

7. The skin contained large circular bumps arranged in regularly spaced rows. It would have been rough to the touch.

8. It had a longer face that some relatives, suggesting that this may have been an adaptation for eating particular plants.

9. It had a short neck for carrying a heavy skull.

10. Its back leg reflexed, suggesting that it could run fairly fast.

COLOR YOURSELF **SMART**
DINOSAURS LATE CRETACEOUS

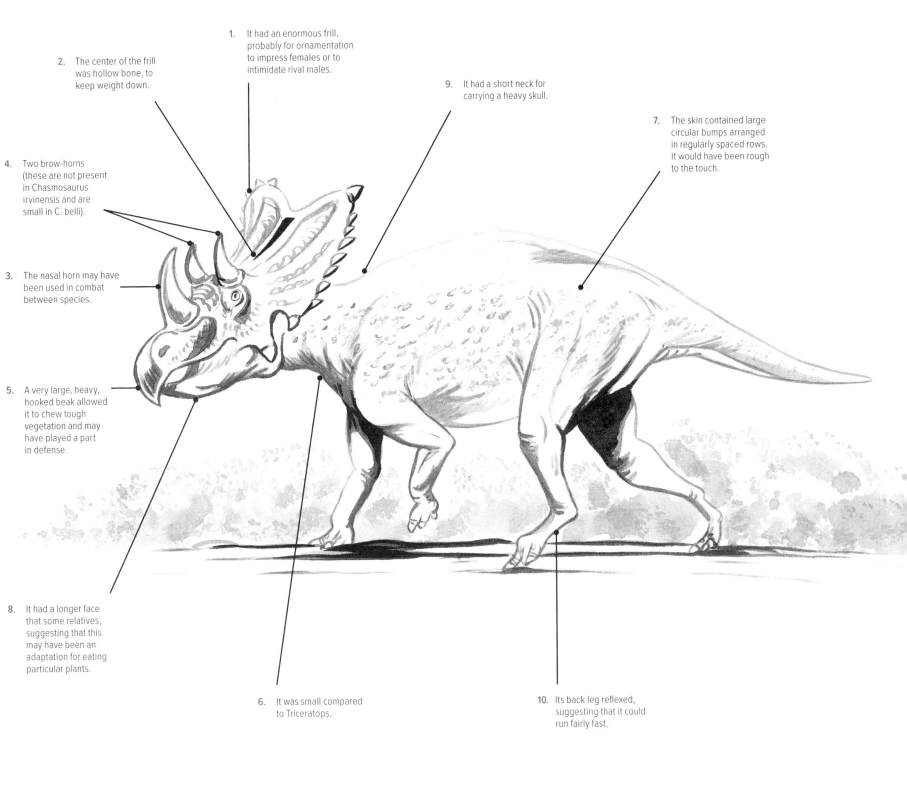

1. It had an enormous frill, probably for ornamentation to impress females or to intimidate rival males.

2. The center of the frill was hollow bone, to keep weight down.

9. It had a short neck for carrying a heavy skull.

7. The skin contained large circular bumps arranged in regularly spaced rows. It would have been rough to the touch.

4. Two brow-horns (these are not present in Chasmosaurus irvinensis and are small in C. belli).

3. The nasal horn may have been used in combat between species.

5. A very large, heavy, hooked beak allowed it to chew tough vegetation and may have played a part in defense.

8. It had a longer face that some relatives, suggesting that this may have been an adaptation for eating particular plants.

6. It was small compared to Triceratops.

10. Its back leg reflexed, suggesting that it could run fairly fast.

Torosaurus | *Torosaurus latus*

Late Cretaceous, U.S.A. and Canada • 68–65 million years ago • 30 feet (9 m) long

TOROSAURUS HAS RECENTLY BEEN AT THE CENTER OF A BIG CONTROVERSY in the world of dinosaur biology. Originally described in 1891, Torosaurus has always been known to be closely related to the better-known Triceratops, owing to its similar arrangement of three horns and a neck frill. However, it differed in having long, straight brow-horns instead of curved ones, and in having a much larger frill at the back of the skull, with two large holes in it, which was lacking in Triceratops. However, in 2009, two scientists surprised the world by suggesting that Torosaurus and Triceratops are the same creature, based on their studies of this group of dinosaurs. Torosaurus is simply the mature form of Triceratops; horns in these creatures are known to straighten with age, and there seems no reason that frills shouldn't grow and change in shape as the animal ages. Unsurprisingly, plenty of experts have challenged the findings, and the debate goes on.

Unaffected by the human world, Torosaurus was a formidable herbivore, with possibly the largest skull-to-body ratio of any animal ever known—its skull was 8.5 feet (2.6 m) long. It would have defended itself by charging (as in the picture), and one of these creatures in a bad mood would have been a match for such predators as Tyrannosaurus, which lived at the same time.

10 THINGS TO REMEMBER

1. It had a small nasal horn (possibly for combat between rivals).

2. It had two very long, straight brow-horns. These were presumably highly effective weapons.

3. It had small eyes (as is typical for a well-armed herbivore that doesn't need sharp vision).

4. It had a powerful beak for cropping, or perhaps grabbing, vegetation.

5. Relatively enormous frill was located at the back of the skull; unlike a number of similar species, it didn't have significant hornlets around the edge.

6. There were two large holes (fenestrae) in the center of the frill on each side. In life, these would have had skin between them that could have been colorful.

7. Males (or females) may have charged each other during combat over territory or mates.

8. Frills are likely to have gotten larger and longer with age.

9. Relatively short legs would have given the animal great stability.

10. A full-body skeleton of Torosaurus has not been recovered, but it is assumed that it was broad to accommodate the intestines.

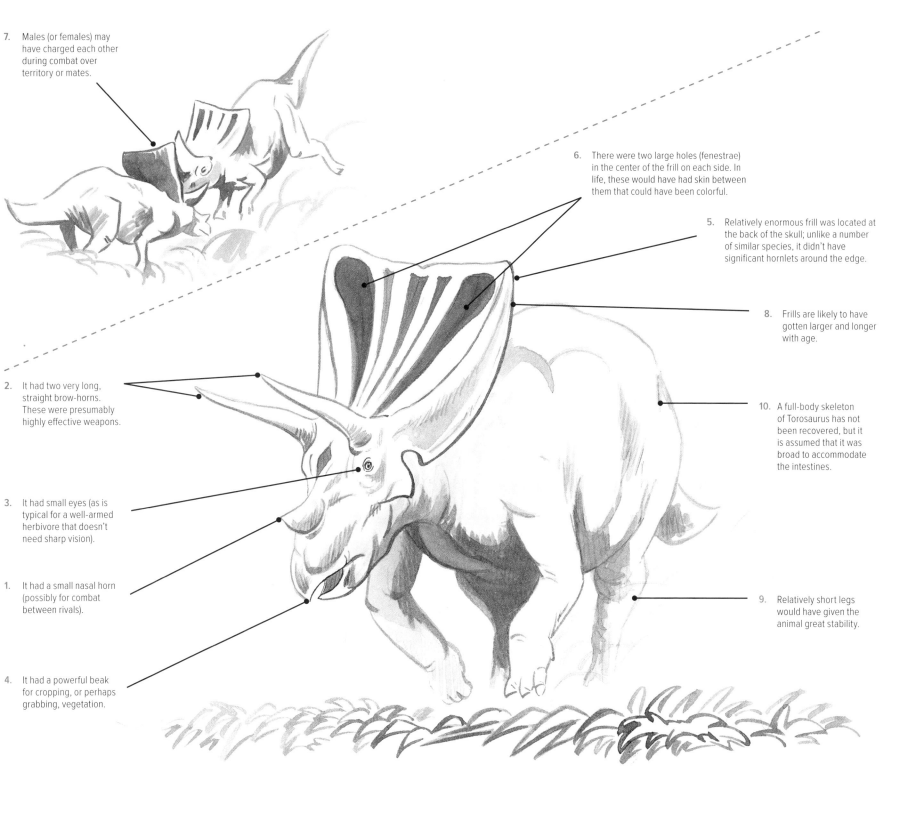

7. Males (or females) may have charged each other during combat over territory or mates.

6. There were two large holes (fenestrae) in the center of the frill on each side. In life, these would have had skin between them that could have been colorful.

5. Relatively enormous frill was located at the back of the skull; unlike a number of similar species, it didn't have significant hornlets around the edge.

8. Frills are likely to have gotten larger and longer with age.

2. It had two very long, straight brow-horns. These were presumably highly effective weapons.

10. A full-body skeleton of Torosaurus has not been recovered, but it is assumed that it was broad to accommodate the intestines.

3. It had small eyes (as is typical for a well-armed herbivore that doesn't need sharp vision).

1. It had a small nasal horn (possibly for combat between rivals).

9. Relatively short legs would have given the animal great stability.

4. It had a powerful beak for cropping, or perhaps grabbing, vegetation.

Pentaceratops | *Pentaceratops sternbergi*

Late Cretaceous, U.S.A. (New Mexico) • 75–70 million years ago • 21 feet (6.4 m) long

THIS REMARKABLE DINOSAUR HAS JUST ABOUT EVERY ADORNMENT in the family book: the large frill typical of a Chasmosaurus and all the same horns as Triceratops, but bigger. You could call it the pinnacle of horned dinosaur evolution, except that it predates those animals mentioned. Perhaps its adornments were simply too many and were dropped in later relatives. Its skull was 10 feet (3 m) long, the largest head known for any land animal in Earth's history—quite a burden to carry.

Pentaceratops is known from just one formation in New Mexico. It is curious that, despite the fact that Triceratops, Pentaceratops, and its kin are among the best-known dinosaurs, they seem to have been relatively localized in the middle of North America. Only one ceratopsid has been found elsewhere so far, in Uzbekistan in Central Asia. Moreover, many have very small ranges, suggesting that they were either geographically isolated or might have become specialized in diet or habitat.

Pentaceratops and its relatives are generally thought to have been herding animals, similar to many of today's herbivores. In some cases, many fossils have been found

10 THINGS TO REMEMBER

1. The nasal horn was long and sharp.

2. It had two large brow-horns, which were long and curved downward. They could have been used in skirmishes between rivals.

3. The skull was enormous, at 10 feet (3 m) long, the largest known for any land vertebrate.

4. Cheek (epijugal) bones stuck out to the side, adding two more "horns"—Pentaceratops means "five-horned face."

5. The frill was also very large, with hornlets on the outer rim, which were presumably just for show.

6. The center of the frill was hollow, as in Chasmosaurus, and was very likely to have been brightly colored and possibly able to change color.

7. The frill was tilted upward, whereas in most relatives it was more or less flat.

8. The legs were flexed.

9. It had a sharp beak, typical of a ceratopsid dinosaur.

10. Massive shoulders contained ligaments to support the skull.

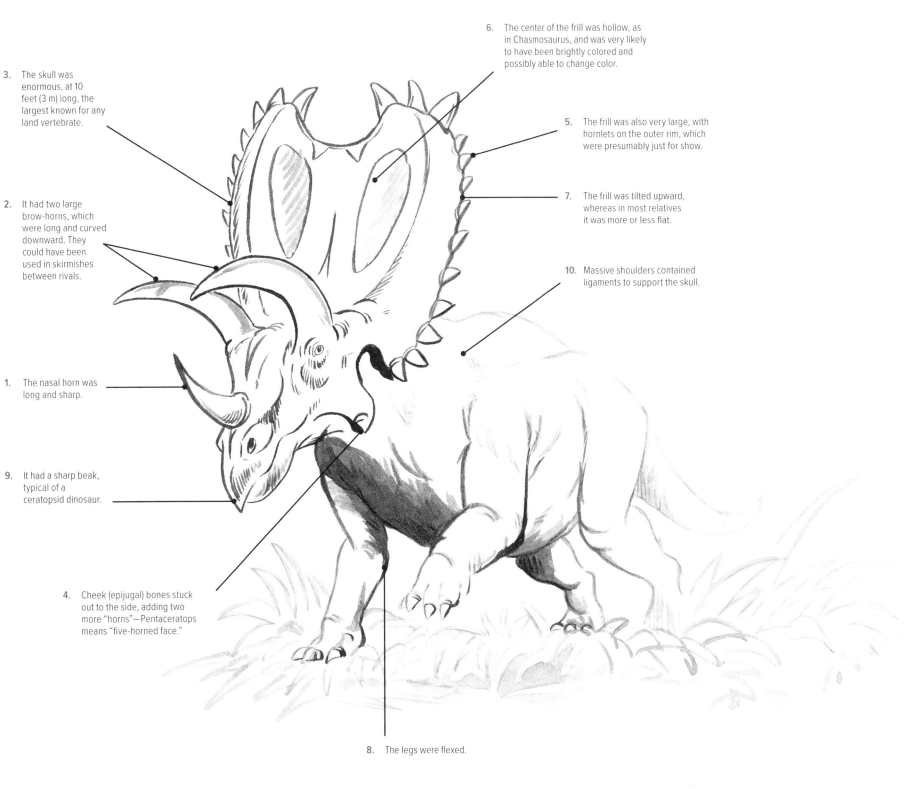

6. The center of the frill was hollow, as in Chasmosaurus, and was very likely to have been brightly colored and possibly able to change color.

3. The skull was enormous, at 10 feet (3 m) long, the largest known for any land vertebrate.

5. The frill was also very large, with hornlets on the outer rim, which were presumably just for show.

2. It had two large brow-horns, which were long and curved downward. They could have been used in skirmishes between rivals.

7. The frill was tilted upward, whereas in most relatives it was more or less flat.

10. Massive shoulders contained ligaments to support the skull.

1. The nasal horn was long and sharp.

9. It had a sharp beak, typical of a ceratopsid dinosaur.

4. Cheek (epijugal) bones stuck out to the side, adding two more "horns"—Pentaceratops means "five-horned face."

8. The legs were flexed.

Psittacosaurus | *Psittacosaurus mongoliensis*

Early Cretaceous, Russia, Mongolia, and China • 125–100 million years ago • 5 feet (1.5 m) long

IF TIME TRAVEL WERE POSSIBLE and you were transported back to the mid-Cretaceous Asia, there's no doubt which dinosaur you would spot first—not a mighty predator, or even a long-necked sauropod. Running away from you would be one of the most abundant dinosaurs known: Psittacosaurus. There were more species (about ten) of Psittacosaurus than of any other genus. They occurred in all habitats, and the genus might have had a longer span of existence than any other. Over 400 skeletons are known, so the overall population must have been in the millions.

The small size and perhaps perceived ugliness of this ancestor of the mighty ceratopsians keep the profile of this herbivore low. Psittacosaurus means "parrot lizard," and it isn't hard to see why. The bizarre skull shows the cheekbones jutting out sideways, as in its later relatives, while the head is oddly rounded, culminating in a beak at the front.

A famous fossil discovered recently sheds light on the family life of Psittacosaurus. The find consists of a perfectly preserved adult adjacent to 34 youngsters, all of which are of the same age. It is likely that a burrow collapsed on the young and their tending adult, killing all instantly. Other specimens preserve groups of Psittacosaurus of mixed ages, suggesting that these animals were sociable.

10 THINGS TO REMEMBER

1. It undoubtedly picked up stones to store in its intestines to help break down plant food. Called gastroliths, these stones soon acquired smooth surfaces and were found in many fossils.

2. Some specimens have long fibers on top of their tails. This has left some to suppose that Psittacosaurus might have had fins and a tail for moving through water, and may have lived at times in the water.

3. It had short arms with three grasping fingers and blunt claws. These might have been used to hold onto trunks and branches.

4. It was bipedal and probably a very good runner.

5. There were no teeth at the front of the skull, and the teeth at the rear were for chopping. It had a blunt, unhooked beak.

6. The lower jaw might have retracted to fit inside the upper jaw. If so, it may have been able to crack open hard nuts.

7. Jutting-out cheekbones (subjugal) are a typical feature of ceratopsians. They had small horns and might have been used in fights.

8. It had a very rounded forehead.

9. The eyes faced partly upward, for reasons that are unclear.

10. The rather long, narrow neck extended reach.

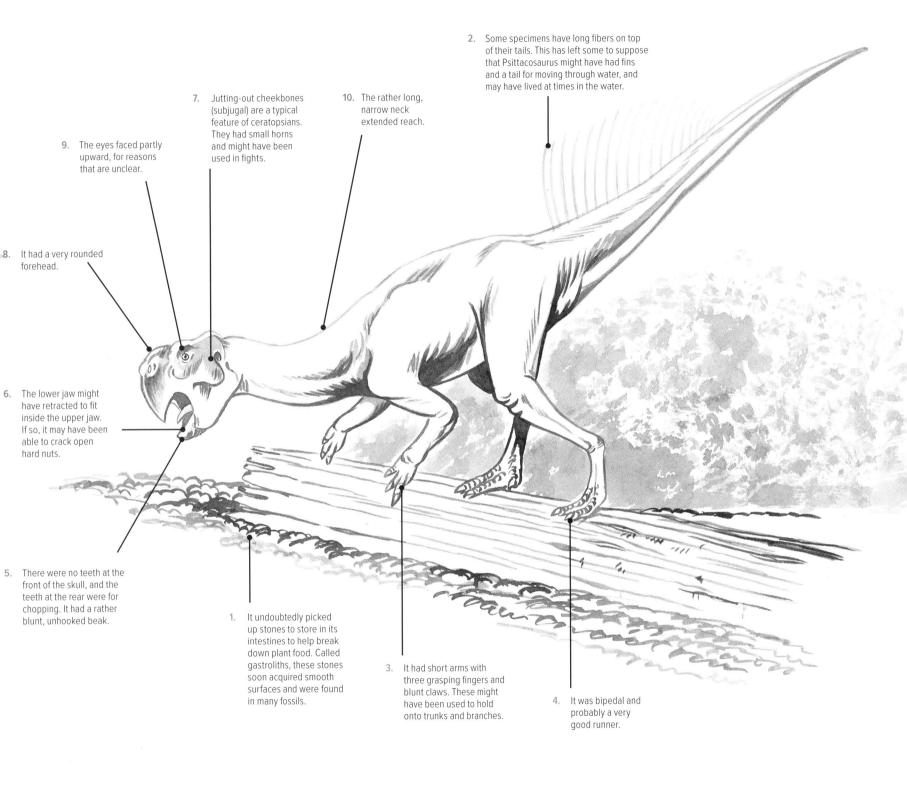

2. Some specimens have long fibers on top of their tails. This has left some to suppose that Psittacosaurus might have had fins and a tail for moving through water, and may have lived at times in the water.

7. Jutting-out cheekbones (subjugal) are a typical feature of ceratopsians. They had small horns and might have been used in fights.

10. The rather long, narrow neck extended reach.

9. The eyes faced partly upward, for reasons that are unclear.

8. It had a very rounded forehead.

6. The lower jaw might have retracted to fit inside the upper jaw. If so, it may have been able to crack open hard nuts.

5. There were no teeth at the front of the skull, and the teeth at the rear were for chopping. It had a rather blunt, unhooked beak.

1. It undoubtedly picked up stones to store in its intestines to help break down plant food. Called gastroliths, these stones soon acquired smooth surfaces and were found in many fossils.

3. It had short arms with three grasping fingers and blunt claws. These might have been used to hold onto trunks and branches.

4. It was bipedal and probably a very good runner.

Lambeosaurus | *Lambeosaurus magnicristatus*

Late Cretaceous, Canada (Alberta) • 75–70 million years ago • 23 feet (7 m) long

LAMBEOSAURUS WAS A MEMBER OF ONE OF THE MOST IMPORTANT groups of Cretaceous dinosaurs, the hadrosaurs. It is hard to think of these animals as anything other than the cattle or wildebeest of the age, since they were slow-witted, gentle, grazing herbivores. They gathered in large herds, all the better to feed a hungry predatory theropod. They were the most abundant dinosaurs alive at the end of the dinosaur age 65 million years ago.

The success of the hadrosaurs was due to their basic design—they could escape by running quickly on two legs and using their thin arms for balance, and they were well adapted for browsing. Their duckbills were ideal for cropping vegetation, and they had large batteries of narrow teeth suited for grinding. Speed and herding were two safety strategies, and they were probably cryptically colored, but if all else failed, they could kick out at a predator with their feet.

Lambeosaurus was an unusual hadrosaur with a strange, helmetlike crest at the back of the skull. This was largely hollow, but housed nasal passages that wound back and forth. Most scientists now think that the crest was used to produce sounds so that the animals could call to each other.

10 THINGS TO REMEMBER

1. It had an elongated snout with a ducklike bill, ideal for reaching and cropping vegetation.
2. The beak projected well beyond teeth
3. A long neck was useful for reaching the upper branches of trees.
4. The tail was kept rigid by bonelike tendons and was laterally flattened, allowing for sharp turns.
5. It had long, thin forelimbs.
6. The long, slim legs allowed for fast running, but it probably usually grazed on four limbs
7. It had vertical wrinkles on its shoulder.
8. It had a bizarre crest on top of its head.
9. Large eyes suggest sharp sight, which was very important for an essentially defenseless herbivore.
10. Nasal passages looped around the crest, so most of the skull was hollow. The crest may have been used to make sounds.

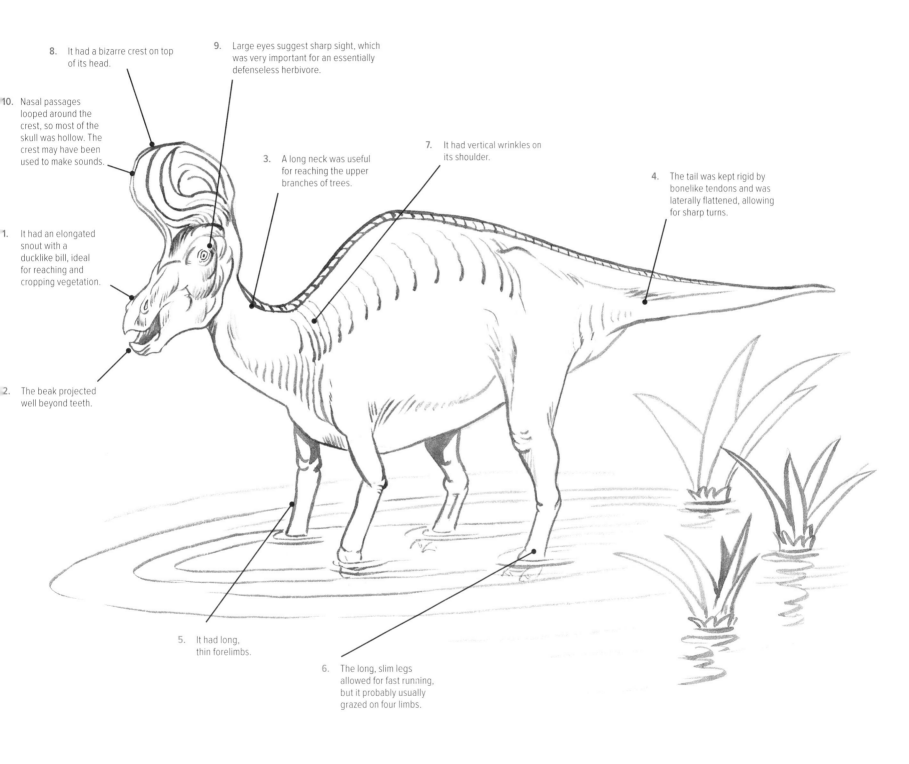

8. It had a bizarre crest on top of its head.

9. Large eyes suggest sharp sight, which was very important for an essentially defenseless herbivore.

10. Nasal passages looped around the crest, so most of the skull was hollow. The crest may have been used to make sounds.

3. A long neck was useful for reaching the upper branches of trees.

7. It had vertical wrinkles on its shoulder.

4. The tail was kept rigid by bonelike tendons and was laterally flattened, allowing for sharp turns.

1. It had an elongated snout with a ducklike bill, ideal for reaching and cropping vegetation.

2. The beak projected well beyond teeth.

5. It had long, thin forelimbs.

6. The long, slim legs allowed for fast running, but it probably usually grazed on four limbs.

Late Cretaceous, Canada and possibly U.S.A. (New Mexico) • 75–70 million years ago • 25 feet (7.5 m) long

ONE ASPECT OF DINOSAUR BEHAVIOR THAT WILL BE FOREVER LOST to time is the sounds that these animals made. There is little doubt that the Mesozoic world was full of loud noises and strange whispers, but we will never get to hear these for ourselves. However, a few animals provide clues about their auditory world, and one of these is the rare and distinctive hadrosaur, Parasaurolophus.

A quick glance at the picture immediately draws the eye to Parasaurolophus's peculiar crest. It is a narrow tubular structure than runs from just above the nostrils along the top of the head; in our picture, the crest is connected by skin to the back of the neck, but in the skeleton, it extends as a tube far beyond the end of the skull. Strangely, the nasal passages run from the nostrils up into the crest and then turn back toward the top of the head, so rather than being solid bone, the crest is hollow and houses nasal sinuses. The most likely function for this crest was, therefore, sound production. Perhaps the animals called to each other in courtship or to declare territory. Maybe a hornlike blast served as an alarm call at an approaching predator.

Fascinatingly, other hadrosaur fossils have revealed well-developed inner-ear bones, suggesting that these animals had a good sense of hearing. This allows us to make an informed guess that these creatures, at least, filled the air with sound.

10 THINGS TO REMEMBER

1. Long, tubular crest ran along the top of the head for 4 feet (1.25 m)

2. The crest had a large surface area and might have been connected to the neck by skin. If so, it might have been used to dissipate or soak up heat, regulating body temperature.

3. The size of the crest varied between individuals. It was distinctive and might have helped distinguish the sexes.

4. The crest was probably colorful.

5. The snout was shorter than in most other relatives and narrower. This might suggest that it browsed selectively.

6. It had shorter front limbs than most other hadrosaurs.

7. Large eyes provided sharp vision.

8. It had a stiff, very broad-based, pointed tail. This probably helped the animal turn.

9. The cheeklike structures kept food in the mouth while the animal was eating.

10. When feeding on two legs, it could reach up to a height of about 13 feet (4 m).

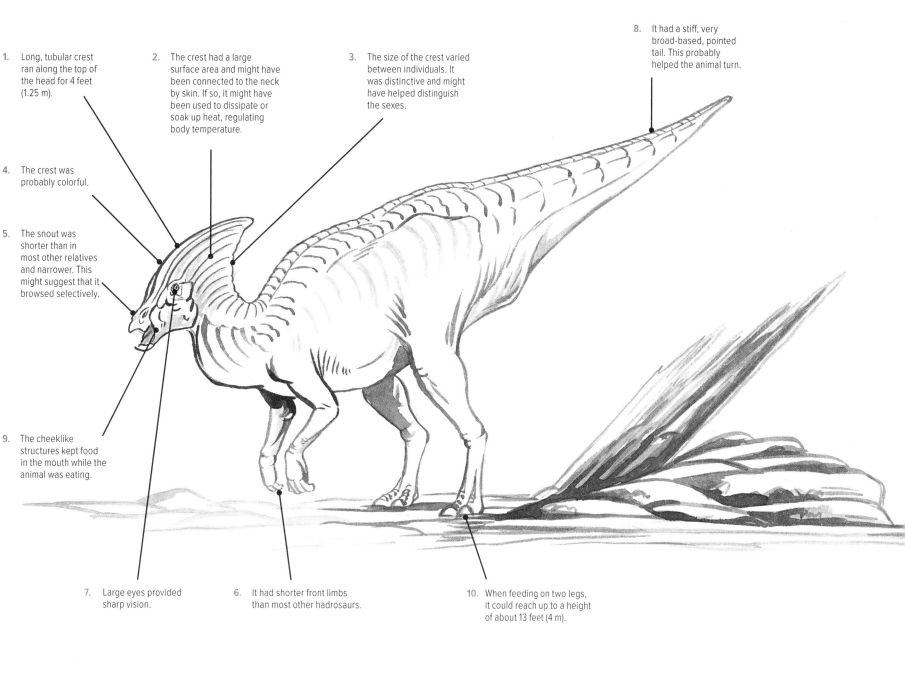

1. Long, tubular crest ran along the top of the head for 4 feet (1.25 m).

2. The crest had a large surface area and might have been connected to the neck by skin. If so, it might have been used to dissipate or soak up heat, regulating body temperature.

3. The size of the crest varied between individuals. It was distinctive and might have helped distinguish the sexes.

8. It had a stiff, very broad-based, pointed tail. This probably helped the animal turn.

4. The crest was probably colorful.

5. The snout was shorter than in most other relatives and narrower. This might suggest that it browsed selectively.

9. The cheeklike structures kept food in the mouth while the animal was eating.

7. Large eyes provided sharp vision.

6. It had shorter front limbs than most other hadrosaurs.

10. When feeding on two legs, it could reach up to a height of about 13 feet (4 m).

Maiasaura | *Maiasaura peeblesorum*

Late Cretaceous, U.S.A. (Montana) • 80–75 million years ago • 23 feet (7 m) long

THE DISCOVERY OF MAIASAURA CHANGED OUR PERCEPTION OF DINOSAURS. Until the pivotal studies on this hadrosaur in the 1970s and 1980s in Montana, we hadn't credited these animals with strong parental care, assuming that they left their eggs to hatch alone. But the multiple eggs, hatchings, juveniles, and adult Maiasaura found painted an entirely different picture.

The most important finding came from studying hatchings that were fossilized next to adults. Some of these youngsters were too big to fit inside their eggs, strongly suggesting that they remained in the nest after hatching. Furthermore, some showed wear on their teeth from eating plant material, but at the same time, their bones were very weak and unsuited to moving around with any vigor, certainly not to feed and graze. The only logical conclusion was that they must have been brought food by a parent visiting the nest. Later studies revealed that young Maiasaura remained in the nest or nesting area for about a year. The abundant nests found in Montana also show that Maiasaura bred in colonies, with the nests about 23 feet (7 m) apart. In the early stages, it is likely that the adults stood guard over the nests, which would have attracted many predators, such as Troodon (see page 104).

Other finds suggested that Maiasaura occasionally gathered in herds of up to 10,000 animals. If so, they would probably have needed to migrate seasonally in order to sustain such numbers.

10 THINGS TO REMEMBER

1. The nest was a mound of dirt, presumably just scraped up from the ground.

2. Each nest contained 30–40 eggs, each about the size of a soccerball.

3. The eggs were arranged in a circular or sometimes spiral pattern, not randomly.

4. The adult(s) didn't incubate the eggs. They were probably surrounded by rotting vegetation, allowing fermentation to keep them warm.

5. Hatchlings had proportionally much larger head than adults, with large eyes—typical for youngsters that depend on parental care. The hatchlings were 18 inches (45 cm) long.

6. Adults brought in vegetation to feed the hatchings at the nest site.

7. The narrow, squared-off beak indicates that Maiasaura was choosy about what it ate.

8. It had a shallow crest across its skull between the eyes. It is likely that this was used for headbutting or for display during territorial combat.

9. It traveled on all fours, but ran on two limbs. It may have made migratory journeys.

10. The feet had hooflike claws.

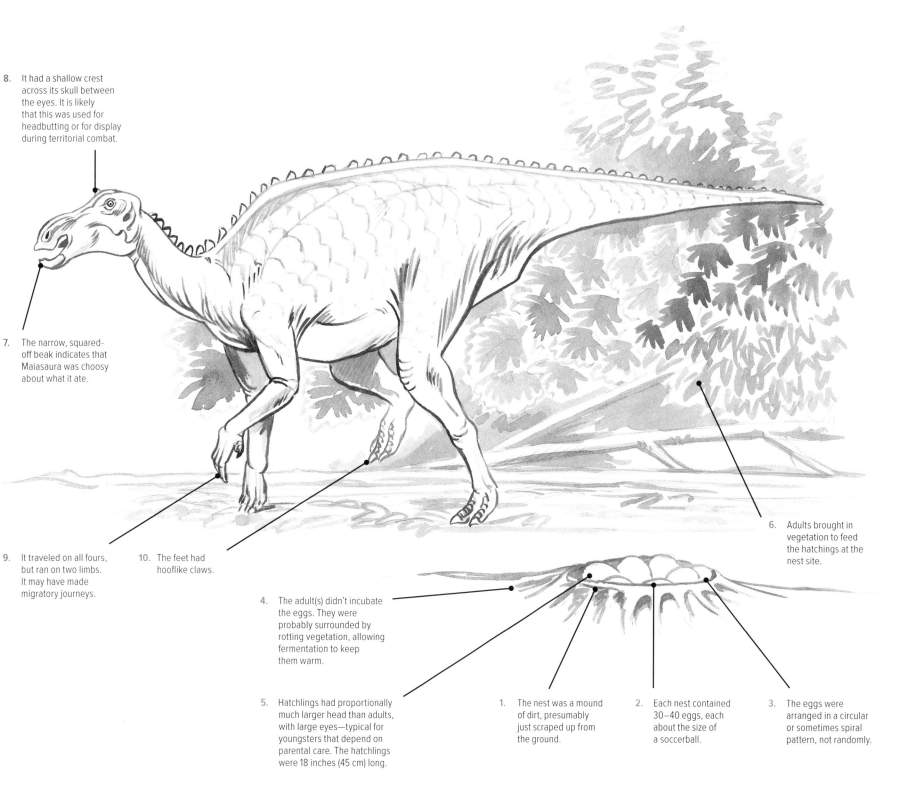

8. It had a shallow crest across its skull between the eyes. It is likely that this was used for headbutting or for display during territorial combat.

7. The narrow, squared-off beak indicates that Maiasaura was choosy about what it ate.

9. It traveled on all fours, but ran on two limbs. It may have made migratory journeys.

10. The feet had hooflike claws.

6. Adults brought in vegetation to feed the hatchings at the nest site.

4. The adult(s) didn't incubate the eggs. They were probably surrounded by rotting vegetation, allowing fermentation to keep them warm.

5. Hatchlings had proportionally much larger head than adults, with large eyes—typical for youngsters that depend on parental care. The hatchlings were 18 inches (45 cm) long.

1. The nest was a mound of dirt, presumably just scraped up from the ground.

2. Each nest contained 30–40 eggs, each about the size of a soccerball.

3. The eggs were arranged in a circular or sometimes spiral pattern, not randomly.

Ankylosaurus | *Ankylosaurus magniventris*

Late Cretaceous, U.S.A. and Canada • 68–65 million years ago • 23 feet (7 m) long

IT IS POSSIBLE THAT ANKYLOSAURUS DEVELOPED the most devastating physical defensive weapon ever known in a land animal: the tail club. This was an extraordinary structure about 1 foot (30 cm) long, made from fused bones, tendons, and plates. It was anchored by seven fused vertebrae at its base, allowing it to be swung without falling off, and it was covered with osteoderms, plates of bone unconnected to the skeleton. Studies have shown that if a large Ankylosaurus swung this macelike club hard enough, it could break the bone of a large predator and probably even do mortal damage.

This, of course, would happen only if a Tyrannosaurus or similar contemporary predator were foolish enough to tackle an Ankylosaurus in the first place. But this would be a waste of energy, because perhaps no other dinosaur in the world was ever so heavily armored. The creature's entire upperside was covered with sharp, oval-shaped bone protrusions attached to the skin and thickened by keratin; in between were smaller bony knobs.

The skull was both small and remarkably solid, with fused bones. It had horns projecting from the top, a series of plates to cover the crown, and a bony rim to protect the eyes. The chances are that, for most of its life, this herbivorous browser was left in peace.

10 THINGS TO REMEMBER

1. The extraordinarily wide body, 6.5 feet (2 m) in width, made it almost impossible to turn over.

2. Plates of armor (bone probably covered with a tough layer of keratin) ran in rows over the top of the body.

3. Side spikes projected outward just above the vulnerable, unarmored underside.

4. The club could be swung and was a potent defensive weapon, from tip to tail. It might also have been useful in display for combat and courtship.

5. Horns projected from the skull. These might have been useful in display for combat and courtship.

6. The rather broad beak indicated that it probably wasn't very selective in the kind of plants it ate.

7. Fairly short legs kept it stable and enabled it to hunker down easily if threatened.

8. It had a very small head for its size. This housed an equally small brain, and it is unlikely that Ankylosaurus was very smart.

9. The rather small eyes suggest that it did not have sharp vision.

10. Complex nasal passages probably indicated a good sense of smell.

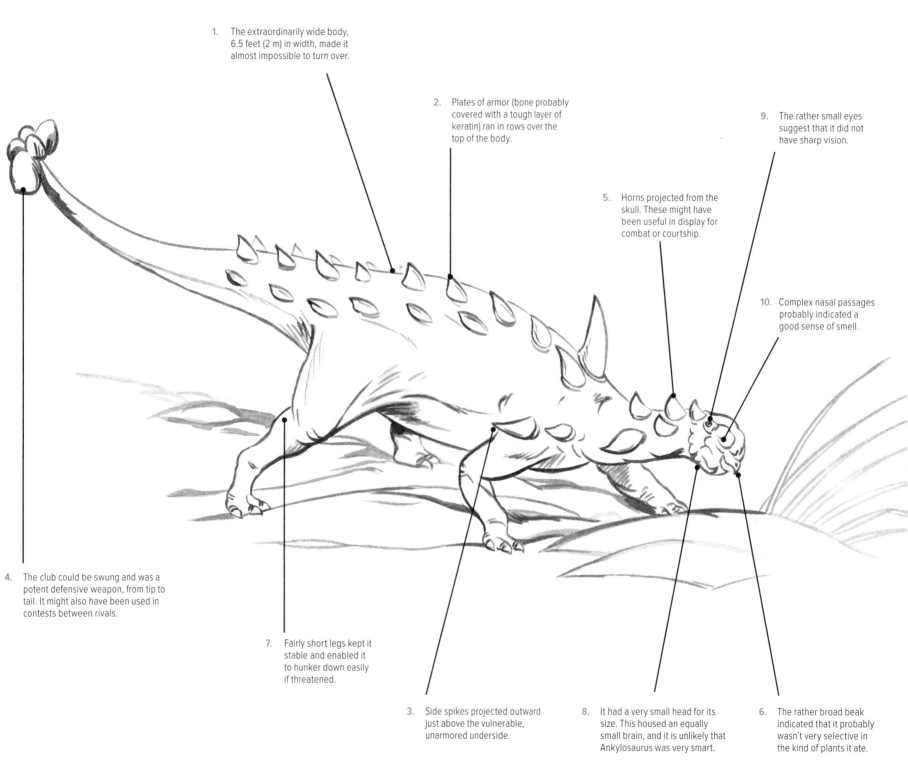

1. The extraordinarily wide body, 6.5 feet (2 m) in width, made it almost impossible to turn over.

2. Plates of armor (bone probably covered with a tough layer of keratin) ran in rows over the top of the body.

9. The rather small eyes suggest that it did not have sharp vision.

5. Horns projected from the skull. These might have been useful in display for combat or courtship.

10. Complex nasal passages probably indicated a good sense of smell.

4. The club could be swung and was a potent defensive weapon, from tip to tail. It might also have been used in contests between rivals.

7. Fairly short legs kept it stable and enabled it to hunker down easily if threatened.

3. Side spikes projected outward just above the vulnerable, unarmored underside.

8. It had a very small head for its size. This housed an equally small brain, and it is unlikely that Ankylosaurus was very smart.

6. The rather broad beak indicated that it probably wasn't very selective in the kind of plants it ate.

Oviraptor | *Oviraptor philoceratops*

Late Cretaceous, Mongolia • 85–75 million years ago • 5.3 feet (1.6 m) long

THE FIRST-KNOWN OVIRAPTOR SPECIMEN was found in the 1920s next to a batch of 15 eggs. At the time, dinosaurs were thought to all leave eggs and nests to their own fate rather than looking after them, and it was assumed that this particular Oviraptor was fossilized in the act of raiding the nest of a local Protoceratops, a type of dinosaur that was abundant in the area. In fact, the name Oviraptor means "Egg Thief," and while no one has yet ruled out a diet including eggs for this poorly known dinosaur, it seems that this initial find was misrepresented. More recently, fossils of closely related species have been found actually on clutches of eggs that unequivocally belong to them, spread out in what is unmistakably an incubating position. So it is pretty clear that "Oviprotector," rather than Oviraptor, might have been a better name.

This is a birdlike dinosaur in shape, and it was almost certainly covered with feathers and had wings and a long tail. Interestingly, paleontologists think that its ancestors were able to fly, but later "gave up" flying, as it wasn't necessary for their lifestyle.

The skull of Oviraptor is very light and is unusual for having downward projections from the palate. These "pseudoteeth" may well have been adapted to crush seeds or even eggs, although the only proven food item for this animal was a small lizard found preserved in its intestines.

10 THINGS TO REMEMBER

1. The skull was extremely light, with air cavities within the bones.

2. The large crest on top of the skull was much too fragile and light to be used for headbutting or other physical displays. Instead, it was probably colorful and boldly marked.

3. Its large birdlike bill was probably used for crushing as well as other feeding, suggesting a broad diet.

4. Outer edges of its beak were highly serrated.

5. The front limbs were modified into feathered wings, but it was still almost certainly flightless.

6. It had a large hand, perhaps for grasping.

7. Its body was covered with feathers.

8. The long tail with a fan of feathers was probably used for balance and steering.

9. The long legs were necessary for running.

10. The eye sockets were only moderately large, and it was probably diurnal.

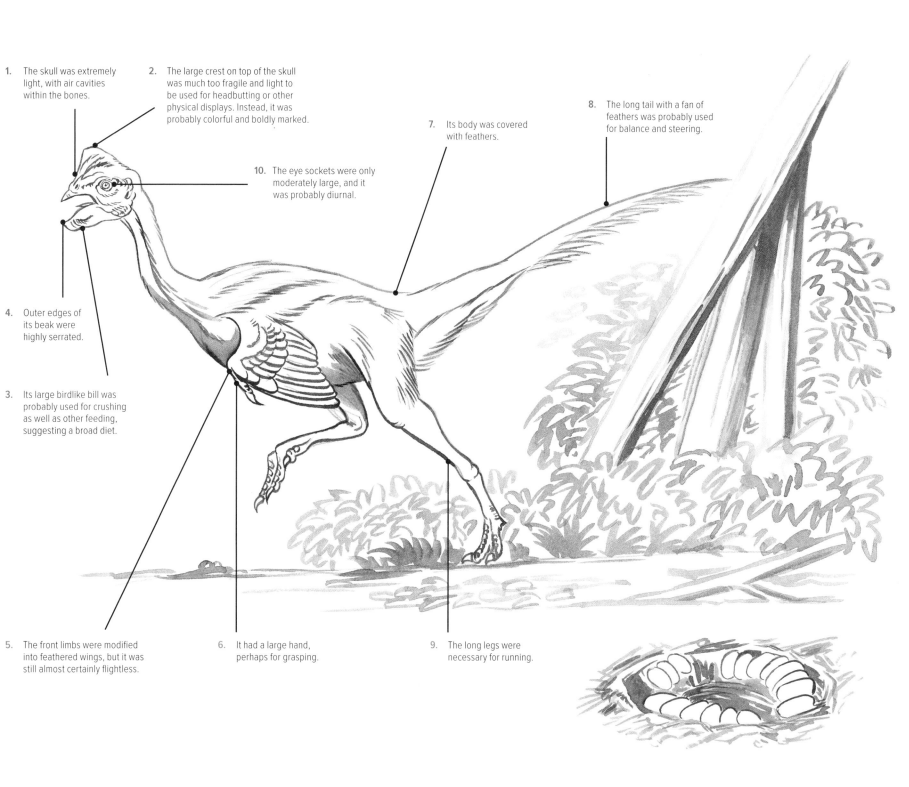

1. The skull was extremely light, with air cavities within the bones.

2. The large crest on top of the skull was much too fragile and light to be used for headbutting or other physical displays. Instead, it was probably colorful and boldly marked.

7. Its body was covered with feathers.

8. The long tail with a fan of feathers was probably used for balance and steering.

10. The eye sockets were only moderately large, and it was probably diurnal.

4. Outer edges of its beak were highly serrated.

3. Its large birdlike bill was probably used for crushing as well as other feeding, suggesting a broad diet.

5. The front limbs were modified into feathered wings, but it was still almost certainly flightless.

6. It had a large hand, perhaps for grasping.

9. The long legs were necessary for running.

Troodon | *Troodon formosus*

Late Cretaceous, U.S.A. (Montana) and possibly Canada • 75–71 million years ago • 8 feet (2.5 m) long

THERE ISN'T MUCH THAT STANDS OUT ABOUT TROODON when you look at it; quite a few other dinosaurs were equally birdlike, with a beak, two swift-running legs, and rudimentary wings. However, what was special about this animal cannot be seen—its large brain. It was probably one of the smartest, if not the smartest, of all the dinosaurs, and as such was probably an advanced predator and opportunist.

Interestingly, Troodon's teeth are leaflike with large serrations (denticles), both of which indicate a herbivorous diet. Most likely it was omnivorous, eating seeds and leaves alongside meat. It would be very unusual for a strict herbivore to have a large brain, because you don't need intelligence to find plants—they are everywhere. Furthermore, Troodon also had very large eyes, possibly giving the most acute vision of any dinosaur, which would be necessary to be a sharp-witted and active hunter. Those same eyes also suggest that it could have been nocturnal, or at least active in twilight.

A few eggs and nests of Troodon have been found. The nests are 3 feet (1 m) wide and were elevated dishes made from soil, with a protective ring keeping them in. Each nest contained 16–24 eggs.

10 THINGS TO REMEMBER

1. Its very large eyes faced forward, probably to give excellent three-dimensional vision.

2. Its numerous teeth were leaf-shaped and serrated, usually a sign of a herbivorous diet.

3. The robust head allowed for killing small game, which could have included fish.

4. It had a long, birdlike beak.

5. It had a typical shape for a raptor, with long legs and a long tail, and was undoubtedly a fast runner.

6. It almost certainly had feathers and probably feathered wings.

7. Its nest was made from mud and was a raised dish 3 feet (1 m) in internal diameter.

8. A protective rim around the nest kept the eggs inside.

9. Eggs were slightly pear-shaped, with the more pointed end facing downward in the nest.

10. It had a large head with a comparatively enormous brain, suggesting high intelligence.

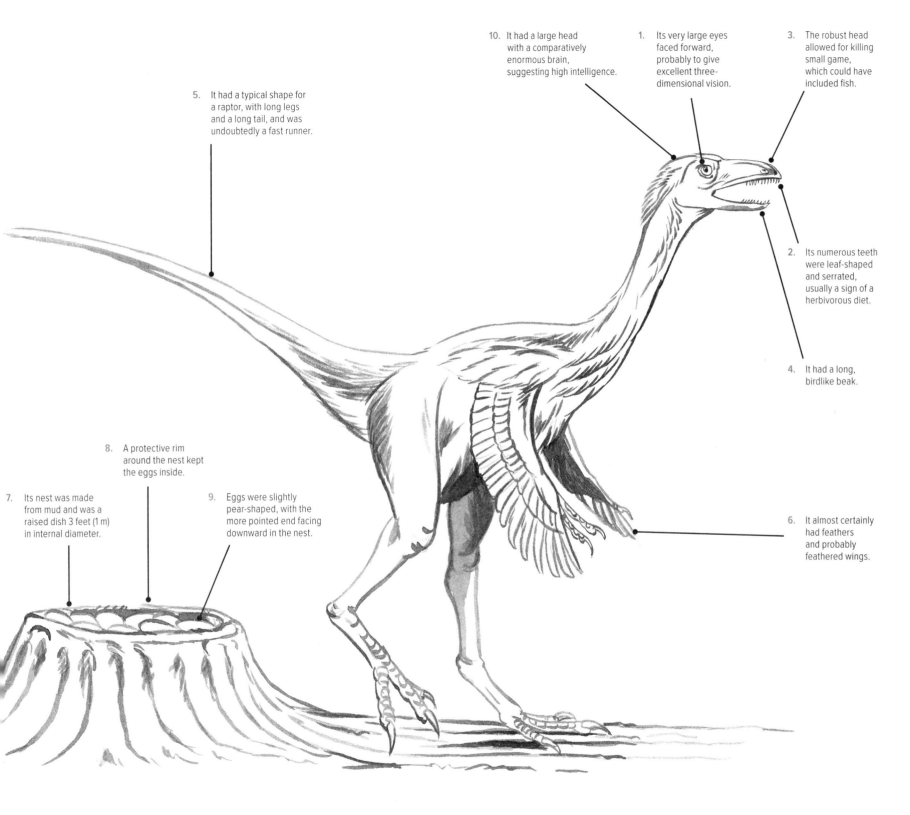

10. It had a large head with a comparatively enormous brain, suggesting high intelligence.

1. Its very large eyes faced forward, probably to give excellent three-dimensional vision.

3. The robust head allowed for killing small game, which could have included fish.

5. It had a typical shape for a raptor, with long legs and a long tail, and was undoubtedly a fast runner.

2. Its numerous teeth were leaf-shaped and serrated, usually a sign of a herbivorous diet.

4. It had a long, birdlike beak.

8. A protective rim around the nest kept the eggs inside.

7. Its nest was made from mud and was a raised dish 3 feet (1 m) in internal diameter.

9. Eggs were slightly pear-shaped, with the more pointed end facing downward in the nest.

6. It almost certainly had feathers and probably feathered wings.

Majungasaurus | *Majungasaurus crenatissimus*

Late Cretaceous, Madagascar • 84–71 million years ago • 20 feet (6 m) long

THE DRAMATIC PICTURE OPPOSITE IS NOT YOUR AVERAGE RECONSTRUCTION of a dinosaur killing another dinosaur. Instead, it depicts something that has made Majungasaurus famous: cannibalism. The two combatants are one and the same species, and there is strong evidence that they attacked and ate each other. There are abundant bite marks on a number of specimens of Majungasaurus that fit nothing else known in the area of Madagascar where they lived, and these bite marks are identical to wounds found on the local sauropods, another frequent prey animal. Of course, it is possible that Majungasaurus scavenged the carcass of its own species, but the savagery of the wounds suggests that fights to the death took place.

It is clear that Majungasaurus was a theropod, with an overall body structure similar to famous carnivores such as Tyrannosaurus and Allosaurus. However, the skulls of Majungasaurus and its near allies are distinctly different from the rest. They are much shorter from front to back and considerably wider, too, suggesting a different method of killing. In many ways they resemble big cats, and it is thought that, instead of slashing and wounding its prey like an Allosaurus, or making an instant deep, deathly wound like a Tyrannosaurus, Majungasaurus was adapted to biting hard into the flesh and holding on as the struggles of the prey gradually subsided.

10 THINGS TO REMEMBER

1. It probably killed by biting into vulnerable areas of flesh, such as the neck, and then holding on until the prey died.

2. The skull was specially strengthened in the nasal area to prevent damage when biting.

3. The lower jaw was more flexible, perhaps to avoid it breaking while the prey was struggling.

4. Outer teeth on the upper jaw were the largest and longest and curved inward to keep hold of prey.

5. The skull was shorter and wider than that of most similar predators.

6. It is known to have attacked and killed its own kind, strongly suggesting cannibalism.

7. The vertebrae are known to have included air sacs, suggesting an efficient, birdlike type of respiration.

8. It possessed a small horn above the eyes, probably used for display or head butting during disputes between individuals.

9. The extremely reduced arm was probably not very useful, except in balance.

10. The legs were not particularly long for this type of predator; it was unlikely to have been very fast.

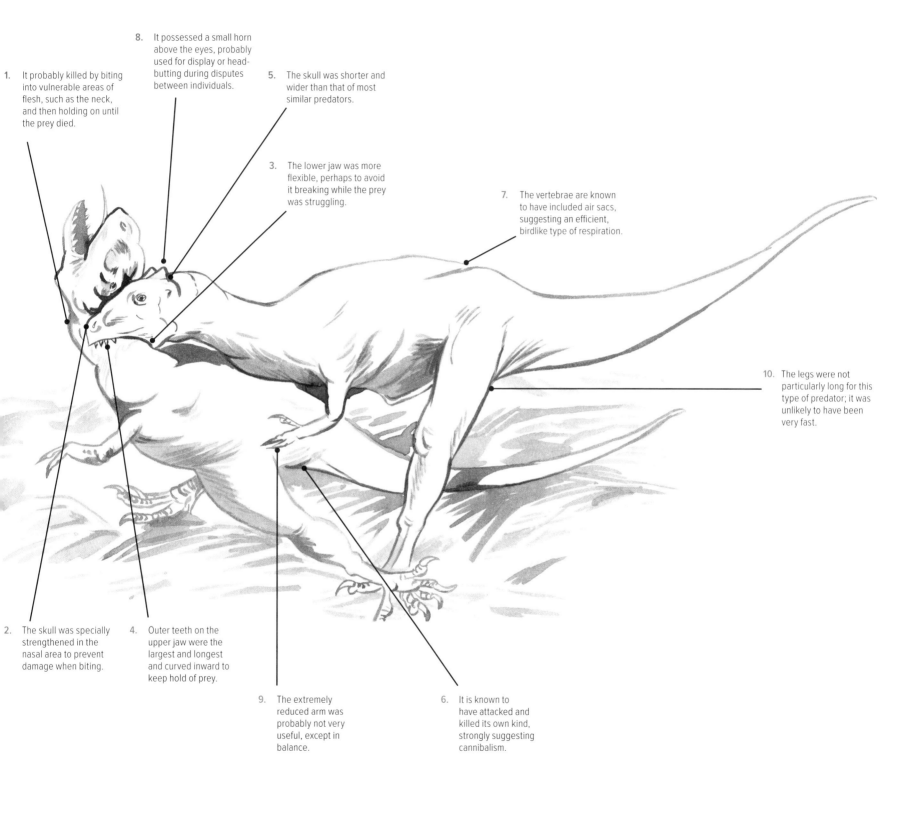

1. It probably killed by biting into vulnerable areas of flesh, such as the neck, and then holding on until the prey died.

8. It possessed a small horn above the eyes, probably used for display or head-butting during disputes between individuals.

5. The skull was shorter and wider than that of most similar predators.

3. The lower jaw was more flexible, perhaps to avoid it breaking while the prey was struggling.

7. The vertebrae are known to have included air sacs, suggesting an efficient, birdlike type of respiration.

10. The legs were not particularly long for this type of predator; it was unlikely to have been very fast.

2. The skull was specially strengthened in the nasal area to prevent damage when biting.

4. Outer teeth on the upper jaw were the largest and longest and curved inward to keep hold of prey.

9. The extremely reduced arm was probably not very useful, except in balance.

6. It is known to have attacked and killed its own kind, strongly suggesting cannibalism.

Saltasaurus | *Saltasaurus loricatus*

Late Cretaceous, Argentina • 71–68 million years ago • 28 feet (8.5 m) long

IT SEEMS THAT THE THE SAUROPOD DINOSAURS were not as big in the late Cretaceous as they had been in their heyday of the Jurassic, the time of the true giants. But they were changing, and one new innovation has been found on the remains of a mainly Cretaceous group called the titanosaurs: armor. On Saltasaurus, this armor consisted of bony plates, called osteoderms, separated from the skeleton and embedded in the skin. This armor probably covered much of the upper surface. It could be a tribute to the evolving power and ferocity of predators that the sauropods' sheer size could no longer fully protect them, and they needed something else.

In fact, Saltasaurus is a small sauropod, with a relatively short neck. It might not have needed to be large or tall, because the late Cretaceous had ushered in the age of flowering plants, and food was abundant. Coprolites (fossilized dung) of titanosaurs have revealed that they ate the recently evolved grasses and other flowers.

The Saltasurus opposite is depicted using its back legs to dig a depression for its nest. A recent find in Argentina has uncovered a Saltasaurus nesting ground, suggesting that these animals laid about 25 eggs and buried them under dirt and vegetation.

10 THINGS TO REMEMBER

1. It used its back legs to dig a burrow for the eggs. These were then covered by soil and vegetation. Eggs were just 4–5 inches (10–12 cm) long.

2. Flowering plants were becoming more common and provided easy nourishment for herbivorous dinosaurs.

3. It had a short neck for a sauropod and may not have needed to reach very high.

4. The armor consisted of bony disks 4 inches (10 cm) in diameter. They might have been covered by small cones.

5. In between the disks were small body protrusions.

6. The long tail had a very narrow end that might have been used as a whip against predators or rivals.

7. It had wide hips and a broad pelvis.

8. It had long arms, so shoulders were as high as the hips.

9. The dinosaur only had teeth at the back of the jaw, and these teeth were blunt.

10. It had a typical small head, to keep weight down at the end of the long neck.

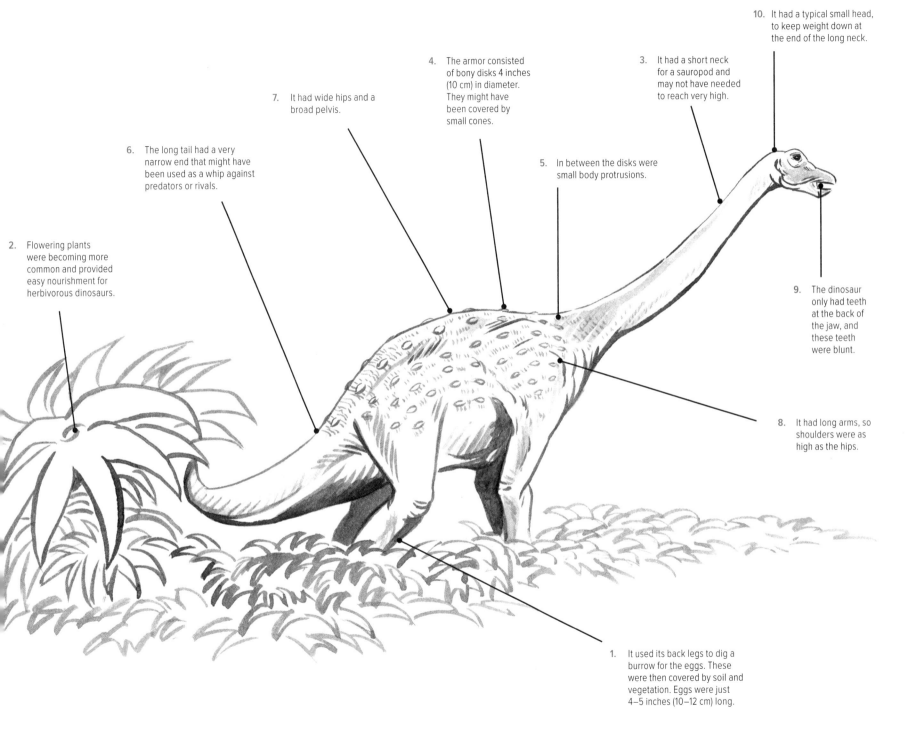

10. It had a typical small head, to keep weight down at the end of the long neck.

4. The armor consisted of bony disks 4 inches (10 cm) in diameter. They might have been covered by small cones.

3. It had a short neck for a sauropod and may not have needed to reach very high.

7. It had wide hips and a broad pelvis.

5. In between the disks were small body protrusions.

6. The long tail had a very narrow end that might have been used as a whip against predators or rivals.

2. Flowering plants were becoming more common and provided easy nourishment for herbivorous dinosaurs.

9. The dinosaur only had teeth at the back of the jaw, and these teeth were blunt.

8. It had long arms, so shoulders were as high as the hips.

1. It used its back legs to dig a burrow for the eggs. These were then covered by soil and vegetation. Eggs were just 4–5 inches (10–12 cm) long.

Therizinosaurus | *Therizinosaurus cheloniformis*

Late Cretaceous, Mongolia • 75–68 million years ago • 33 feet (10 m) long

THIS REMARKABLE DINOSAUR WAS A TRUE ODDITY, and it is also something of a mystery. The enormous claws, which were up to 2 feet (0.7 m) long in some individuals, dominate its appearance, yet we do not know for certain what their function was. It seems unlikely that they were used as weapons, since they would have been unwieldy. They could have been used to attract or capture mates; males had larger claws than females. Or perhaps they were used for food gathering in some way. The claws have reminded some scientists of the hands of giant sloths, which use their long claws to pull the branches of trees so that they can reach high-growing leaves. This does seem to be the most likely explanation. Of course, the claws could have served all three functions.

One thing does seem certain: Therizinosaurus was a high browser. The pelvis was large and angled sideways so that the animal could lean upward effectively, and the extremely long neck would have allowed it to reach 23 feet (7 m) or more. The broad trunk and relatively short tail support this notion.

For a long time, no one knew what a Therizinosaurus was—in fact, the first guess from just a few bones was that it was a turtle! The small head and long neck suggest a sauropod, but this animal actually has the distinctive three-digit hand of a theropod—one of the few herbivorous species of that kind.

10 THINGS TO REMEMBER

1. The extremely small head was typical of a herbivore.

2. The long neck was an adaptation to high browsing.

3. It had an amazingly long arm, which reached 11.5 feet (3.5 m) in some specimens.

4. The most obvious feature was enormous claws, the largest known for any land animal. They were up to 2 feet (0.7 m) long, not including the horny sheath that probably covered them.

5. The claws were slightly curved, but probably weren't used for defense. They might have been used to pull down branches.

6. It was bipedal, which was typical of a theropod.

7. It had a pot belly and wide pelvis, the latter allowing the animal to balance when leaning upward.

8. The comparatively short tail was rigid and useful for balancing.

9. Oddly, it had four weight-bearing toes on each foot. Most theropods had only three.

10. It has been found in lush, well-watered habitats.

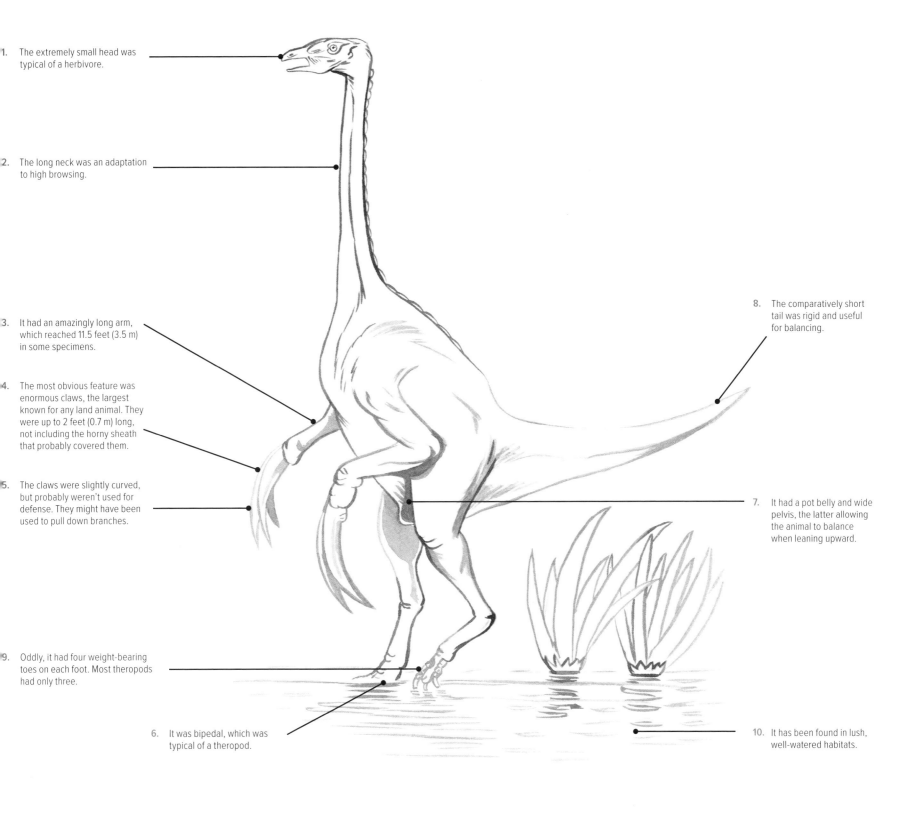

1. The extremely small head was typical of a herbivore.

2. The long neck was an adaptation to high browsing.

3. It had an amazingly long arm, which reached 11.5 feet (3.5 m) in some specimens.

4. The most obvious feature was enormous claws, the largest known for any land animal. They were up to 2 feet (0.7 m) long, not including the horny sheath that probably covered them.

5. The claws were slightly curved, but probably weren't used for defense. They might have been used to pull down branches.

6. It was bipedal, which was typical of a theropod.

7. It had a pot belly and wide pelvis, the latter allowing the animal to balance when leaning upward.

8. The comparatively short tail was rigid and useful for balancing.

9. Oddly, it had four weight-bearing toes on each foot. Most theropods had only three.

10. It has been found in lush, well-watered habitats.

Centrosaurus | *Centrosaurus nasicornis*

Late Cretaceous, Canada (Alberta) • 71–68 million years ago • 16.5 feet (5 m) long

THIS ANIMAL WAS THE RHINOCEROS OF THE CRETACEOUS ERA, with its long and vertical nasal horn. However, if there were a time warp and it did battle with a modern-day rhino, there is no doubt which animal would win. Centrosaurus was a little larger than a rhinoceros, at 16.5 feet (5 m) long when adult, compared to the largest rhino at 15 feet (4.6 m), but it was considerably heavier. It also had a better array of headgear than a rhino, with a frill at the back of the skull studded with hornlets on its outer rim, plus small horns above its eyes. Even so, it would have been an interesting contest to witness.

Evidence suggests that Centrosaurus was a sociable animal, gathering in herds at least some of the time—bone beds with hundreds, possibly thousands of skeletons have been found. The bone beds may have resulted from some kind of disaster, such as a drought concentrating many animals in one spot, but this doesn't rule out herding as the norm.

Additionally, Centrosaurus had a social life. The horns and frills would have afforded some protection from enemies, but their probable secondary function was to intimidate and impress in equal measure. It might be a fanciful depiction, but the animal opposite could have been bellowing a challenge to any rival in the area to take part in a contest of headgear.

10 THINGS TO REMEMBER

1. The large, almost straight nasal horn was 5 feet (1.5 m) long.

2. The vertical nature of the horn suggests that Centrosaurus would have struck an enemy from below with a thrusting forward movement.

3. Two small horns over the eyes might have been display features.

4. The rim behind the skull is smaller than in some relatives and was probably used mainly as an adornment for combat or courtship.

5. Frills varied and were not always symmetrical.

6. It had small hornlets around the edge of the frill (these give Centrosaurus its name of "pointed lizard").

7. The frill contained two large holes (fenestrae) to keep down the weight.

8. Thick limbs supported the heavy body.

9. The jaws were extremely strong and adapted to exploit coarse plant material.

10. In territorial combat, it may have assumed intimidating postures like this to challenge rivals.

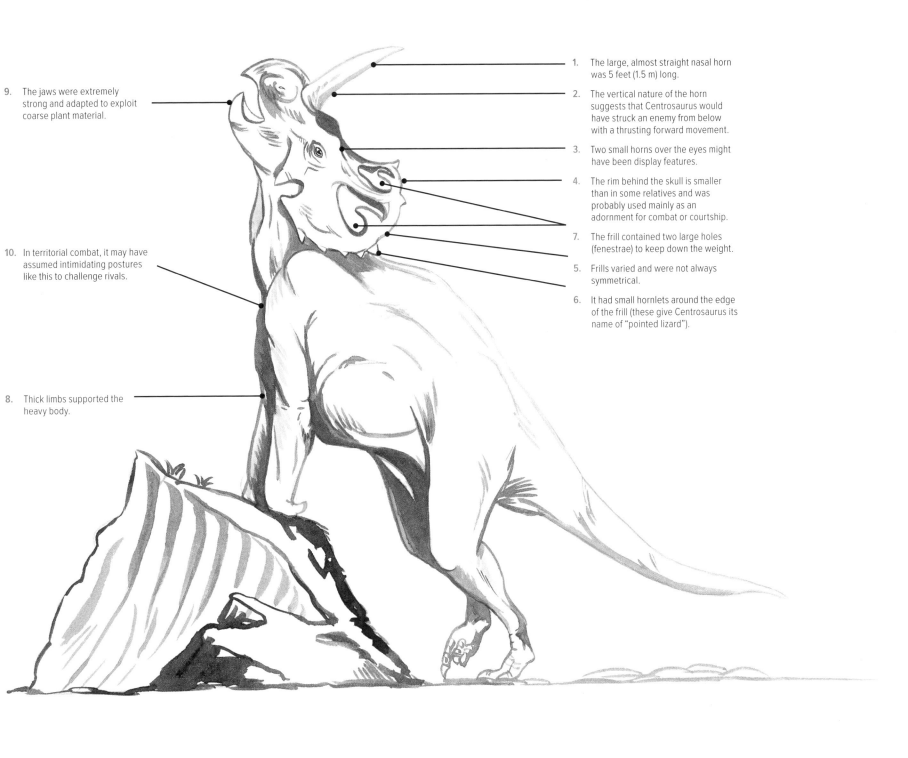

9. The jaws were extremely strong and adapted to exploit coarse plant material.

10. In territorial combat, it may have assumed intimidating postures like this to challenge rivals.

8. Thick limbs supported the heavy body.

1. The large, almost straight nasal horn was 5 feet (1.5 m) long.

2. The vertical nature of the horn suggests that Centrosaurus would have struck an enemy from below with a thrusting forward movement.

3. Two small horns over the eyes might have been display features.

4. The rim behind the skull is smaller than in some relatives and was probably used mainly as an adornment for combat or courtship.

7. The frill contained two large holes (fenestrae) to keep down the weight.

5. Frills varied and were not always symmetrical.

6. It had small hornlets around the edge of the frill (these give Centrosaurus its name of "pointed lizard").

DINOSAURS IN FULL COLOR

Plateosaurus

Eudimorphodon

Herrerasaurus

Saurosuchus

Coelophysis

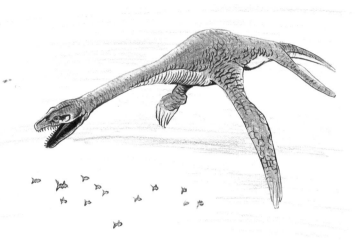

Rhomaleosaurus

Massospondylus

Gongxianosaurus

Scelidosaurus

Megalosaurus

Mamenchisaurus

Huayangosaurus

Diplodocus

Stegosaurus

Kentrosaurus

Brachiosaurus

Camarasaurus

117

Archaeopteryx

Iguanodon

Allosaurus

Ouranosaurus

Gastonia

Deinonychus

Utahraptor

Microraptor

Sinosauropteryx

Amargasaurus

Tupandactylus

Archaeoceratops

Argentinosaurus

Spinosaurus

Quetzalcoatlus

Carcharodontosaurus

Tyrannosaurus

Velociraptor

Triceratops

Protoceratops

Pachycephalosaurus

Torosaurus

Chasmosaurus

Pentaceratops

Psittacosaurus

Parasaurolophus

Lambeosaurus

Maiasaura

Ankylosaurus

Troodon

Oviraptor

Majungasaurus

Saltasaurus

Therizinosaurus

Centrosaurus

QUIZ

1. What are the most abundant "ghosts" at Ghost Ranch in New Mexico, U.S.A.?

2. Which part of the world does the famous predator Velociraptor come from?

3. Which dinosaur is unusual in that some adults are twice as big as others?

4. Why couldn't Scelidosaurus chew?

5. Which animal gives us a clue that the original dinosaurs might have evolved in South America?

6. How did the hatchlings of Massospondylus move differently from the adults?

7. Which two features immediately suggest that a pterosaur is primitive (early in the fossil record)?

8. What was the name of the fearsome, crocodile-like creature of the Triassic that had the ability to run?

9. Which predator is thought to have been the main enemy of Triceratops?

10. Which was the first dinosaur to be described scientifically?

11. Which was the first group of dinosaurs to become extinct, as far as we know?

12. Known since 1891, what do some scientists now think that Torosaurus actually is?

13. In a battle between Centrosaurus and a modern-day rhinoceros, which would have won?

14. Which dinosaur is thought to have had the longest neck, proportionally?

15. Which dinosaur is generally regarded as the largest of all time?

16. On what continent was Kentrosaurus found?

17. Why does the name Oviraptor not really fit the animal?

18. What feature of Huayangosaurus points to it being related to Ankylosaurs?

19. Which famous dinosaur seems to have nested in colonies and cared for its young?

20. How long could a Brachiosaurus live?

21. What feature of the skeleton of Camarasaurus (and other sauropods) was an adaptation for saving weight?

22. How did Allosaurus kill its prey?

23. What were the most abundant herbivorous dinosaurs of the late Cretaceous?

24. In pterosaurs, which bone is vastly extended to form the leading edge of the wing?

25. Name two dinosaurs with "sails" on their backs.

26. In what era did Gastonia live?

27. Which dinosaur has the largest skull of any animal known on Earth?

28. Which dinosaur had four wings?

29. Which was the first nonavian dinosaur discovered to have feathers, albeit primitive ones?

30. Which birdlike dinosaur is thought to have been the most intelligent of all?

31. What odd function has been suggested for the peculiar "mane" of Amargasaurus?

32. What feature does Archaeoceratops lack that most of its later relatives had?

33. How do we know what Saltasaurus and its fellow titanosaurs ate?

34. Which dinosaur had a bite equivalent to the strength of a hyena's?

35. What was the (astonishing) wingspan of Quetzalcoatlus?

36. One of the largest of all land predators, Spinosaurus had an unexpected favorite diet. What was it?

37. What is the meaning of the name Carcharodontosaurus?

38. What terrifying dinosaur of the late Cretaceous had teeth that were 1 foot (30 cm) long?

39. How big was a Stegosaurus's brain?

40. What is unusual, and unsettling, about the feeding habits of Majungasaurus?

41. One of the world's most famous fossils has a Protoceratops locked in combat with which predator?

42. How is Chasmosaurus believed to have impressed members of the opposite sex?

43. Which ferocious dinosaur of the early Cretaceous had a single claw 8 inches (20 cm) long?

44. There are more known species of Psittacosaurus than of other dinosaur. How many are there?

45. How many vertebrae did Diplodocus have in its tail?

46. What is thought to have been the function of the strange crest on Parasaurolophus?

47. Where did plesiosaurs lay their eggs?

48. What famous fossil is considered to be the earliest-known bird?

49. What famous anatomical quirk protected Ankylosaurus from any kind of enemy?

50. How fast could an Iguanodon run?

51. Which dinosaur is thought to have had the largest claws of any known land animal?

52. What is the standout unusual feature of Pachycephalosaurus?

QUIZ ANSWERS

1. Coelophysis
2. Mongolia
3. Plateosaurus
4. It could only move its jaws up and down, not sideways.
5. Herrerasaurus
6. They were totally quadripedal. Adults could walk on two or four legs.
7. Extended toothed jaw and long tail
8. Saurosuchus
9. Tyrannosaurus
10. Megalosaurus
11. Prosauropods
12. A full-grown Triceratops
13. Centrosaurus
14. Mamenchisaurus
15. Argentinosaurus
16. Africa
17. The name means "egg thief," but the eggs adjacent to the first fossil discovered were probably its own.
18. Its broad, armor-plated skull
19. Maiasaura
20. 100 years
21. Bones contained cavities
22. It wounded large animals by slashing them from the side with its head and jaws.
23. Hadrosaurs
24. The fourth digit (finger) of the hand
25. Ouranosaurus, Spinosaurus

26. Early Cretaceous
27. Pentaceratops
28. Microraptor
29. Sinosauropteryx
30. Troodon
31. The bones clattered together to make a noise.
32. A horn
33. From their coprolites
34. Deinonychus
35. 33–36 feet (10–11 m)
36. Fish
37. Shark-toothed lizard
38. Tyrannosaurus
39. The size of a walnut (on an animal 21 feet/ 6.5 m long)
40. It was occasionally cannibalistic.
41. Velociraptor
42. By its frill
43. Utahraptor
44. About 10
45. 80
46. Making sounds
47. Nowhere—it gave birth to live young.
48. Archaeopteryx
49. Its tail club
50. 15 miles per hour (24 km/h)
51. Therizinosaurus
52. The dome on the top of its skull.